Nashua Public Library

Enjoy this book!
Please remember to return it on time
so that others may enjoy it too.

Manage your library account and
discover all we offer by visiting us
online at www.nashualibrary.org

Love your library? Tell a friend!

The Mayans Among Us

Migrant Women and Meatpacking on the Great Plains

Ann L. Sittig *and*
Martha Florinda González

University of Nebraska Press
Lincoln & London

All photos provided by the author.

Publication of this volume was assisted by a grant from the
Friends of the University of Nebraska Press.

Library of Congress Cataloging-in-Publication Data
Names: Sittig, Ann L., author. |
González, Martha Florinda, author.
Title: The Mayans among us: migrant women and
meatpacking on the Great Plains / Ann L. Sittig and
Martha Florinda González.
Description: Lincoln: University of Nebraska Press, [2016] |
Includes bibliographical references and index.
Identifiers: LCCN 2015037372
ISBN 9780803284616 (cloth: alk. paper)
ISBN 9781496208477 (paper: alk. paper)
ISBN 9780803285811 (epub)
ISBN 9780803285828 (mobi)
ISBN 9780803285835 (pdf).
Subjects: LCSH: Guatemalans—Nebraska—Social
conditions. | Maya women—Nebraska—Social conditions. |
Immigrant women—Nebraska—Social conditions. | Packing
house workers—Nebraska. | Guatemala—Social conditions.
| Guatemala—Emigration and immigration. | Nebraska—
Social conditions.
Classification: LCC F675.G82 S57 2016 | DDC
305.48/6872810782—dc23 LC record available at
http://lccn.loc.gov/2015037372

Set in Arno Pro by L. Auten.

This book is dedicated to the Mayan women and the Ladino soldier in Nebraska who gave us their stories, to all the meatpacking employees, to all the immigrants living and working in the United States, and to all the Nebraskans who welcome us in their communities, in the hopes that together we can continue building the "Good Life" in Nebraska.

Contents

Illustrations

Maps

Preface

My name is Martha Florinda González. I am a Guatemalan Mayan Q'anjob'al woman living in Nebraska. From 1954 to 1996 my country suffered a civil war in which more than 200,000 Mayan indigenous people were massacred, their villages burned and razed, and their bodies discarded in hidden mass graves. After the Peace Accords were signed in 1996, my people began trying to rebuild our millenarian culture and country, searching out our indigenous beliefs and customs as a stronghold to begin the long journey back to peace.

This long civil war impoverished communities and triggered endless waves of emigration to other countries from the 1970s and on. The war depleted our natural resources, destroyed the physical terrain that had been modified for war, and halted all social services. Emigration emptied our country of most of the remaining young men who had survived the civil war, but were consequently subsisting below the poverty line. Full of optimism and hope for a better future, some crossed two borders to reach El Norte[1], the North, in search of work and sustenance for their families back home. Some men managed to establish themselves in the United States and began sending *remesas,* or remittances to their families in Guatemala. Years later, because of severe poverty, the women decided to join the men. As the women and mothers of the house, they left Guatemala, and oftentimes their children, to help their families survive by working in the United States.

We Mayans arrive and build community in the United States. Many live in Nebraska meatpacking cities, working at the plant to subsist and sending money home to maintain relatives in Guatemala. We speak one of the more than twenty Mayan languages as our first language. Many Mayan women do not speak Spanish, or speak it with difficulty as a second language, because they didn't have access to school, and this makes learning English very difficult. Some of the women work many hours at the plant, or raising their children and keeping house, but learning English is one of their future dreams.

One day, in 2005, Ann Sittig, the coauthor of this book, came to one of our community churches because she had been researching Mayan women in Guatemala, only later to realize many of us were also living in the same state that she is from, Nebraska. We told her our immigration stories because we want to share our lives with the Americans, to help them understand why we are here and who we are. Sometimes we fear the *americanos*, Americans, don't want us here, but maybe if they knew our stories they would understand why we need to work and live here, and they could accept our presence in their communities.

During the journey to El Norte, and after our arrival, we live in community because we need one another. We Mayans like to live in extended kin groupings, and we try to stay abreast of what's happening with our friends and neighbors so that we can help one another. We like to practice our Mayan traditions that have been passed down throughout the generations while discovering and learning about the cultural diversity in the United States. Our ancestors taught us that it is only through listening to one another that we can participate in council, that is, partaking of the mat, or *pop*, interweaving our stories and opinions to craft a woven reality that belongs to all of us as one, a practice reflected in our Mayan book of creation, the *Popol Vuh*.[2] Not communicating with our American neighbors is the hardest part of living in the United States because we come from a community-centered culture.

Since we cannot tell our American neighbors our stories ourselves, because we don't speak or write English, Anna and I have transcribed the Mayan women's stories in an effort to acknowledge the dignity and importance of their lives in contemporary U.S. society. Over the past ten years, between birthing children and teaching, we have recorded the stories in Spanish, translated them to English, and collected them here for you, dear reader. We have explained our Mayan childhood in Guatemala, the civil war, the Peace Accords and processes, the subsequent migration in search of economic stability, life in our new Nebraska communities, our work at the meatpacking plant, and we simultaneously interlace our beautiful, millenary culture throughout the narratives. Anna and I fill in the blanks between the Mayan women's accounts of their life experiences to explain more about Guatemala and the way our Mayan and Nebraskan cultures fit together to make a new hybrid reality, that of the U.S. Mayan woman immigrant.

We, the Mayan women living in Nebraska, would like to share our stories with you. We love our new communities, and we work hard for the money that provides the daily sustenance for our families here and assists with celebrations of special occasions for our families in Guatemala. We are thankful to be alive and to have work. We are also thankful to be able to provide our tiny children with a life that is better than the one we led in Guatemala. And we thank you, dear reader, for taking the time to care enough about us to read our stories.

—*Martha Florinda González*

Acknowledgments

A special thanks to the UFCW workers in all of the cities; they all went above and beyond the call of duty to inform us regarding their many, diverse, multiethnic employees. We also extend our heartfelt thanks to the community members who opened their doors to explain their cities' dynamics to us. We appreciate the Benedictine monastery in Schuyler, and all its staff, especially the administrator, Father Thomas Leitner, who encouraged the dialogues and opened the monastery for group meetings with the women, and also Brother Andrew Fuller, the bookstore manager. We thank Helaine Rampley of the Shasta College Writing Center for her infinite assistance with the bibliography and her constant support of our project. A special thanks to Candace Byrne, Justina Bacon, Wolfgang Rougle, and María del Rocío Guido for early readings and editing of the book. We thank Metropolitan Community College and the Title VI grant that launched the research, and the endless support that Barbara Velazquez, Mary Wise, and Jose Badillo have given to our research. Thanks to Cindy Gonzalez of the *Omaha World Herald* for information regarding the Nebraska Mayan community. We extend our sincere appreciation to María Isabel Velázquez and her colleagues at the University of Nebraska who received us so warmly, extending much support for our project in its early phases. We especially thank our parents and families for supporting us in all of our academic endeavors. And lastly, we would like to extend our appreciation to Elaine Carey at St. John's University and the anonymous readers who critiqued this book and suggested revisions, and our most profound gratitude goes to Matt Bokovoy, Heather Stauffer, Ann Baker, Gretchen Albers, and the University of Nebraska Press for their kindness, dedication, and effort in taking this book to publication.

Introduction

My name is Ann Sittig, I am from Nebraska, and I teach Spanish at Shasta College in Redding, California. After completing my doctoral coursework in Spanish language and literature in Spain, I accepted a position teaching Spanish at Metropolitan Community College (MCC) in Omaha, Nebraska, in 2001. At that time MCC and Little Priest Tribal College in Winnebago, Nebraska, were conducting research under the auspices of a U.S. Department of Education grant, comparing Mayan and Native American Winnebago cultures and seeking out places of intersection, and I researched Mayan women's literary voice. Nobel laureate Rigoberta Menchú is the predominant voice, and Calixta Gabriel Xiquín and Maya Cu are two exquisite Mayan poetesses with powerful words, visions, and messages. The results of this research can be seen at http://www.mayanwomen.com.

At MCC, we conducted research in the United States, and then traveled to Guatemala and Belize to meet with Mayans. However, one day, back in Nebraska, I was driving through the Latino neighborhood of south Omaha when I saw two Mayan Guatemalan women walking down the street in *cortes*, Mayan woven skirts. I remember pulling my car over and just sitting there for a moment, stunned, as I watched them head into a local shop. Here we were, traveling all the way to Guatemala and Belize to "study" the Mayans, when evidently they were living right here among us! A few weeks later, driving through the numerous, small, meat-packing cities, I stopped in a secondhand shop and overheard a couple speaking Spanish with the unmistakable Mayan lan-

guage inflections. When I went right up to them and incredu-
lously asked if they were from Guatemala, they hesitantly answered
that yes, they were. After sharing my experiences and interest in
Guatemala, they excitedly authenticated that yes, they were also
Mayan, and there were many more Mayans, just like them, living in this and the neighboring communities, and working in the
meatpacking plants.

This quest for the Mayan women's literary expression had taken
a new turn; I sought out a local Catholic mass in one of the meatpacking cities, and from the pulpit I bid the women to tell me their
stories. That day I met Martha Florinda González, and in 2005
we eagerly began our collaboration to gather the oral history of
contemporary Mayan women living in Nebraska and working
in the plants. This book is an effort to share the Mayan women's
stories and their contribution to U.S. society. It is also homage
to the invisible, to the immigrants who often live in quite difficult physical and economic circumstances while contributing the
unsung labor that keeps the U.S. economic machine in motion.

Martha was the first person who invited me into her home and
agreed to be interviewed. We sat down at her kitchen table, and
after a few of my questions she halted the whole process, saying,
"Anna, I don't know how interested you are really going to be in
my story. I really didn't suffer very much in Guatemala. My story
isn't like the other women's stories. I've had a lot of opportunities."

This saddened me. She felt her story would only interest me,
an Anglo, educated woman, if it were a story of hardship. This
perhaps exemplifies the way the Mayan women in Nebraska perceive educated middle-class Anglo women, and equally as important, the way they feel Anglos perceive and interpret their race,
social class, and lives. Throughout this project the Mayan women
I have met display immense humility, tranquility, and overflowing hospitality. They are so generous, dedicating time from their
one free day a week, from their strenuous labor at the meatpacking plant or from taking care of their children, to graciously tell
their migration story.

Further along in the process I tried to orient Martha as well, when she came to present to students at MCC, letting her know they might yawn or fall asleep because they worked by day and studied at night. I also warned that the other guest speaker was known to be a quite boisterous feminist, but she assured me she was not nearly as sheltered as I might have imagined, that she had seen it all, serving on the Peace Commissions in Guatemala with people from all levels and from many different countries.

This was the beginning of our two-way journey, to get acquainted and write this book to honor the Mayan women living in Nebraska and working in the meatpacking plants. We may have different jobs or family situations, but all of the women involved in this project have one thing in common: we value and believe in basic human rights such as shelter, employment, education, and health care, for ourselves, our children, and our families.

This book includes excerpts from interviews with five Mayan women and one Ladino[1] man, all of them living in Nebraska cities where they (or their husbands) work in local meatpacking plants. The interviews were conducted in Spanish, which none of us speak as a first language except for the Ladino man, so communication is multilayered. The women tell their accounts in a repetitive and circular way, similar to how ideas are expressed in their Mayan languages and in Spanish, but also because they are relaying their message in a second language they don't manipulate very confidently.

From the outset Martha has been crucial to the culmination and organization of information, and the book would not be possible without her insight and editorial input. Martha received her bachelor's degree and completed her coursework toward a master's degree in political science from the Universidad Rafael Landívar in Guatemala City. She has served on the Coordinating Commission for Indigenous Women, the Technical Commission for Negotiations, and on the Commission for Women, facilitating the dialogues between government and civil society, particularly rural residents, indigenous people, and labor unions.

As well, she has participated in the Peace Processes. As a female Mayan leader in Guatemala, and now in her Nebraska community, Martha is trusted by the women, who followed her lead in opening up to me. I gathered and taped the interviews of both the women and community members, transcribed and translated them, and Martha and I spent numerous hours in person and on the telephone, drawing together all the information we accumulated and presenting it in a way that is respectful, informative, and accurate in regard to transnational Mayan culture, employing a language that has repeatedly been translated and retranslated to ensure accuracy in both meaning and expression.

Juana, Manuela, Lucía, María, and José are the others interviewed. Juana and Manuela are from the Huehuetenango region of Guatemala. Juana is a twenty-six-year-old mother of four and has worked at a local plant for three years. Manuela has worked at two different local plants for a total of five years. She is twenty-five years old, and a mother of two. Lucía, María, and José are from the Quetzaltenango region of Guatemala. Lucía is a twenty-nine-year-old mother of four who has worked at three different local plants for a total of six years. María has no children, is twenty-seven years old, and has worked in meatpacking for a little over a year. José is a thirty-eight-year-old father of three, and he has been working in a local plant for four years.

This project began as a meeting between women from different countries, cultures, races, and sectors of society. Our interviews culminated in group dialogues to decipher the psychological, sociological, and economical wounds left by war, a life of poverty, emigration, and residence in a new country with an unknown language. In our group meetings we found we all shared a desire to develop ourselves to our highest potential, although the Mayan women often prioritize the well-being of their children over individual aspirations. Whether their children are here or back home with parents or other relatives, the Mayan women's main goal is to make lives for them that are better than their own childhoods in Guatemala.

Martha and I support the Mayan women by listening to and transcribing their stories, hoping that our writing and presentations will attract attention to their situation and increase understanding and communication within communities in Nebraska, throughout the United States, and back home in Guatemala. We feel the Mayan women give us their stories because they wish to help build a common understanding, leading to change and improving the situation that Guatemalan Mayan immigrants face both once they arrive in the United States and throughout their migrations.

As this book project took form, many community members expressed interest and were willing to contribute their opinions and experiences revolving around the Mayan immigrants' presence in their cities. We have included excerpts from interviews with social service employees, former plant employees, English as a second language (ESL) instructors, meatpacking union officials, religious and educational leaders, community members, and a local sheriff in order to give a more complete picture of life in the meatpacking city.

Throughout the interview process the Mayans only gave their first names, stating they did not want their names or location revealed in the book. Some of them are undocumented and live in fear of losing their jobs or being deported. Others could suffer violent retaliation, including death, upon their return to Guatemala if their identities were connected to their stories—a result of the hostile civil divisions caused by the war. Therefore, we do not give their exact names, their present or past locations, or the names of the community members who gladly stepped forward to talk about the Mayan presence in their cities, all in an effort to protect them.

The Mayan women interviewed are mostly from the western Guatemalan highlands, a mountainous, rural region. They were not directly victimized by the war in their communities, but some nearby communities were razed. The book begins with a glimpse of the Mayan women's childhoods and lives in Guatemala, and then

1. Map of Guatemala, courtesy Bill Nelson.

details the more than thirty-year civil war that left approximately 200,000 indigenous victims, who were often buried in mass graves. The war—especially the resulting economic devastation—was the main impetus for the emigration to the United States from Guatemala that began in the 1980s. The signing of the Peace Accords in 1996 and the postwar processes put in place to begin rebuilding the country are noted, as is Martha's participation as a Mayan indigenous woman collaborating on indigenous postwar committees. The harrowing experiences of many Guatemalan men who made the journey to El Norte are discussed. The women tell about their new lives in the United States, working in the meatpacking plants and living in Nebraska cities raising their children, while simultaneously struggling with their documentation requirements. Local Nebraskan community members also share their opinions about the newcomers and the effects they have had on their cities. The book concludes with a vision for a shared future in transnational, trilingual, tricultural communities.

Chapter 1 details the Mayan women's lives in Guatemala before immigrating to the United States, noting their Mayan indigenous dress, subsistence farming, daily life, customs, and sustenance. The women describe their families, work experiences, gender inequity, educational opportunities or lack thereof, and their language use. They share accounts of the intense poverty that led them to leave Guatemala in pursuit of economic security for themselves and their relatives.

Chapter 2 explains the events leading up to the Guatemalan civil war, and José narrates his experience as a soldier in the army. The Historical Clarification Commission report *Memory of Silence* detailed the atrocities of the civil war. Intense economic and social issues needed to be addressed in the aftermath of the war, and Martha details her work on numerous postwar reorganization and rebuilding committees. War and the ensuing poverty caused the interviewees to feel that their only option was to leave Guatemala.

Chapter 3 covers the journey to El Norte, detailing how each interviewee struggled with the decision to emigrate, the journey, and border crossing. The problems of obtaining travel visas and the documentation needed for employment once they arrived in the United States are outlined. Kinship networks facilitated their arrival and search for housing and employment. Some of the Mayan women have left children behind, and they describe building a new life in the United States while supporting transnational family members.

In Chapter 4 the Mayans describe their community life in Nebraska, which is centered on religious practice and supported by social service agencies that serve and guide them in their new land. Mayan ritual and practice, once suppressed, organically reemerges. The transformation of transnational religious practice is summarized. Learning a new way of life in the United States challenges the Mayans, and they note how consumerism varies across borders and defines their new reality. Officials at local community, educational, and law enforcement agencies detail how the Mayans impact their organizations and the services they offer. All the interviewees note how trilingual communication impedes integration in their communities.

Chapter 5 tells of the Mayan presence in the meatpacking plants and provides an overview of beef production in Nebraska. Mayans share their personal hiring process and experience working in the plants, and a union official gives more details about the workings inside the packinghouse. A discussion of meatpacking worker rights follows. Meatpacking income fuels the remittances that ensure survival for transnational families, but workload fluctuations along with external market forces impact their incomes. The changing Latino demographics in Nebraska meatpacking cities are outlined, highlighting the way immigrants trigger changes in the educational system and other social service systems.

In the conclusion a Mayan-Nebraskan community vision of a harmonious trilingual and tricultural life, one with more immigrant involvement in their new cities, emerges. The Mayan circular nature of time is a model for noting our interdependence and taking it into consideration as we each devise a lifestyle to sustain ourselves on this planet. The book closes by urging much-needed immigration reform in the United States, questioning how it will affect the Mayans and how Nebraska communities will continue adapting to the constant change caused by the incoming labor force that fuels its corn- and beef-driven economy.

Five years after we conducted the interviews that are the core of this book, I again pull into the Benedictine monastery in Schuyler, the place where we often met to compile the women's stories. When I open the car door the air is fresh, different from that in the city of Omaha. It's a very hot Nebraska summer evening, seemingly even too hot for birds to be joyful, but they are still here and singing, regardless of their backdrop. Peace at last. I pull open the heavy main door and breathe in all the old familiarity of this monastic sanctuary. I weave my way through the long silent hallways, peeking in at the chapel, noting the soft flow of the fountain, and continue on, silently greeting each of the old, familiar religious statues as I seek out my retreat quarters where we will work. Upstairs I swing open the door to my room, and am pleasantly greeted by the strong scent of corn, growing now, its silvery hair protruding from the tightly encased ears on stalk upon stalk. The cornfields encircle the entire monastery. This is home for me. I have driven through miles and miles of Nebraska cornfields, neat rows, linear, tall and assured, reminiscing about my teenage summer job corn detasseling, walking between rows and yanking the tassels from the looming stalks of one corn variety so that it could be cross-pollinated by other rows, producing seed corn. During my entire stay at the monastery, each time I open the door to my room, my sanctuary, I am still greeted by the smell of corn. I breathe in deeply, savoring the fragrance. All my life, when I tell people I am from Nebraska, most of them groan and say, "Ugh. I've driven through there. Interminable. Miles and miles of corn," but there is nothing like prying the tight, canvas-like husks enclosing the golden fruit to the side, parting the delicate, lemony yellow silk, and pushing your nose in to experience the smell of a fresh ear of this corn.

La milpa, corn. In Guatemalan Spanish, influenced by the many Mayan languages spoken both before and after the conquest, cornfields are referred to as *la milpa*. Martha and some of the other women have told me of their deep connection to corn, the base of the *tortilla*, the flat corn patty. Maize is the Guatemalan staple food.

In the evening I take a quick walk about the monastery lake, mosquitoes nipping at my heels, and water bugs flitting about making tiny waves, just to show off their exuberant talents. The humidity is lying in the air like a wet shower curtain at your side. Saint Benedict, the bronze version, spreads his arms wide to encase us all. Benedictines pray to the place where all religious beliefs hopefully intersect, coming together as one and the same.[2] Off the main entrance a statue of the Virgin Mary is housed in her own little private amphitheater. She is enshrouded in a cornhusk that makes a safe haven for her. She stands upon the earth, balancing on a bronze globe with representations of the sun and the moon on it, here at this monastery, so surprisingly placed in the midst of these rolling plains. The plaque reads, "Mary, Fruit of New Creation. Pray for us." On the memento card, Anselm Grün, a German Benedictine monk, explains the symbolism of Mary, enshrouded in a cornhusk, standing upon the planet:

> Mary emerges from a corncob. Corn has its origin in Mexico. For the Indians, corn is not only a symbol for prosperity and happiness, but for the cosmos and the evolution of humanity. . . . Mary, the mother, from whom God's son took flesh, represents also mother earth. . . . Looking at Mary I trust that my life will not remain fruitless. I see how the ear of corn breaks open, how the husks—symbol for the old—fall away, and how Mary emerges as the cob. My body with all that blooms and withers within, with all that grows and all that breaks, is the place in which the new fruit is ripening, that God brings forth within me.

This quote mirrors another passage we read in my Spanish class at the community college while studying Rigoberta Menchú and her efforts to remedy the plight of all indigenous peoples of Guatemala, and I shared it with the Mayan women the day we first met. In full synchronism it is also about corn, a central symbol in Mayan cosmology and subsistence. We share it with you too, in the hopes that it will resound, even if you aren't from a place where corn is so central. Menchú explains: "We always see ourselves as an ear of corn. If the ear of corn is missing one kernel, that absence will always be noticed, there's an empty space, because that kernel has a special place. We are individuals and social activists at the same time." Menchú writes that when her native Quiché land is wounded, she feels it as a wound inflicted on humanity, and she laments that the world has lost this sensitivity, a loss resulting in impunity, thousands of casualties, and a disregard for life in Quiché, because humanity no longer feels it as its own wound. She encourages a return to sensitivity: "Humanity has to recover that sensitivity to avoid wars and conflicts. The indigenous cosmic vision should be a contribution to humanity's sacred thinking."[3]

It is the aftermath of war that has brought Mayan immigrants to Nebraska. They travel for days, crossing Guatemala, and then Mexico, with no luggage, sleeping only a few moments when possible, nervously wondering if they will make it alive, until the luckiest finally arrive safely. Many of them quickly find out that life in cities such as Miami, Houston, Chicago, or Los Angeles is too expensive, that there are too many other immigrants grappling for the few jobs that the undocumented can do. However, they often have a relative who tells them about the "good life" in Nebraska, where there are numerous rural cities with meatpacking plants needing low-wage laborers, so they relocate. It is easy to stay once they arrive; they are met by the familiar sight of the corn that has been the center of their daily sustenance, growing as in the Guatemalan rural highlands. The fields filled with corn, the open skies and clean air, and small city living, with few people, all remind them of home.

The corn is what resounds with them, and so they stay, and they work preparing the corn-fed beef that Nebraska supplies to markets near and far. They begin carving out and trimming down their own individualized version of the American Dream, and they send home as much money as possible to keep relatives subsisting. Martha says when people in the meatpacking city ask her where they are from, she answers, "We're from Guatemala," and her oldest son, poking a stalwart thumb into his chest, counters: "*I'm* from the United States." Wide-eyed, she shrugs her shoulders, and admits, "He is from the United States, and he is proud of that. That's what they teach him at school. He's *American*. And he's also a Nebraskan. And at home, we teach him he's a Q'anjob'al Mayan from Guatemala too." This new trilingual, tricultural identity existing within and on the periphery of the meatpacking plants in rural Nebraska rose up out of the state's longtime corn producing, cattle feeding, and meat processing. This book tells about the weaving together of these three different cultures in rural Nebraska because of transnational migrations prompted by poverty, which stems from neoliberalism and its creation of free trade agreements that benefit strong economies while diminishing social services and thus augmenting poverty among the poor in countries with underdeveloped economies and a lowered standard of living.

Abbreviations

ALMG	Academy of Mayan Languages of Guatemala
BPI	Beef Products Inc.
BSE	Bovine Spongiform Encephalopathy, more commonly known as mad cow disease
CAFTA	Central America Free Trade Agreement
CEH	Historical Clarification Commission
COMG	Council of Mayan Organizations of Guatemala
COPMAGUA	Coordinator of the Mayan People's Organizations of Guatemala
DHS	Department of Homeland Security
E. coli	Escherichia coli
EGP	Guerrilla Army of the Poor
EPA	Environmental Protection Agency
ESL	English as a Second Language
FAMDEGUA	Association of Relatives of the Detained-Disappeared of Guatemala
FAR	Rebel Armed Forces
HR	Human Resources
IBP	Iowa Beef Processors
ICE	Immigration and Customs Enforcement
IIRIRA	Illegal Immigration Reform and Immigrant Responsibility Act
INS	Immigration and Naturalization Service
IOM	International Organization for Migration
IUCM	Instance of Unity and Consensus Maya

MCC	Metropolitan Community College in Omaha, Nebraska
MINUGUA	United Nations Verification Mission in Guatemala
NAFTA	North American Free Trade Agreement
OEA/Propaz	Organization of American States
ORPA	Revolutionary Organization of the Armed People
OSHA	Occupational Safety and Health Administration
PDH	Human Rights Procurator (or Prosecutor)
UFCW	United Food and Commercial Workers
UPMAG	The Mayan People's Union
URNG	Guatemalan National Revolutionary Unit
USCIS	United States Citizenship and Immigration Services
USDA	United States Department of Agriculture
VAWA	Violence Against Women Act
VWP	Visa Waiver Program
WIC	Women, Infants, and Children Program

Guatemala

Life before Emigration

The Mayans interviewed emigrated from the hamlets and municipalities of the western highland provinces such as Huehuetenango,
San Marcos, and Quetzaltenango. Most cities have paved streets
and transportation systems, while some of the outlying villages
still have winding dirt roads. Some adobe houses are topped by
commonplace straw-thatched roofs, and others have tin or tile
roofs. Subsistence farming is the main industry, with some min-
ing and handicraft production. Maize is the most prevalent crop,
but the rich soil enhances wheat, potato, barley, alfalfa, and bean
cultivation. In warmer areas, coffee, sugarcane, tobacco, chili peppers, yucca, *achiote*—a seed to color food—and fruits are grown.
Families cultivate crops on small parcels of land, taking advantage of the abundant rain and fertile soil. Those with a stable economic situation also raise animals, mostly sheep.

The women speak Q'anjob'al, Mam, and K'iche', three of the
many Mayan languages spoken in Guatemala. Those who attended
school also speak Spanish. The women sometimes refer to their
Mayan languages as *dialecto*, or "dialect," because that is how it is
often referred to in Guatemala, although most educated Mayans
do not use this term, knowing it is a denigratory construct coined
by the dominant class, to diminish and erroneously categorize
their more than twenty languages as mere "dialects" of Spanish.
In Nebraska, the Mayan women often refer to their languages as
"Mayan," in general, because most Americans may not be aware
they speak languages other than Spanish. In Guatemala the indigenous often state they are "Maya Q'anjob'al" or "Maya Mam,"

and so on, referring to their particular indigenous identity in a show of self-respect. Being stripped of one's actual ethnic group and language, or having it misrepresented or misdefined, has led to the internalized colonization and racism that many Mayans strive to overcome.

According to Michael Coe in *The Maya*, the Mayan language linguistic family is made up of numerous interrelated yet mutually unintelligible languages, but classification is difficult. Very early there was one Mayan language, Proto-Mayan, which split into Huaxtecan, Yucatecan, Western, and Eastern Mayan. In the Western Mayan group they spoke Greater Cholan and Greater Kanjobalan, which later developed into Cholan, Tzeltalan, Kanjobalan. The Eastern Mayan group spoke Mamean and Greater K'iche'an. Languages largely define Mayan groups and ethnicity.[1]

As small children, the Mayan women began helping out with household and farming chores as soon as capable. Some of them lived in small villages remote from the main cities, but they would regularly go to the centers on market days to shop and socialize. They walked for hours to the market if they couldn't afford the public transportation provided by crowded local trucks. They recall dancing to marimba music at town festivals, but for the most part, living in poverty meant they got up early and started working, stoking the outdoor fire for cooking, and mixing the *nixtamal*, corn masa, to make tortillas for the family, before everyone set out to work, planting and harvesting corn and other staples, or tending the small herds of sheep. Some had to haul water from pumps in the middle of the village or from rivers and lakes, carrying it long distances home.

Mayan Dress

Since childhood the women wore their *traje*, the Mayan clothing that varies according to indigenous ethnic regions and language groups, and exemplifies the country's more than 50 percent Mayan citizenry with multicolored, artistic designs. The Mayan women have worn a woven blouse or *huipil*, and a woven skirt or *corte,* while living in Guatemala, but in Nebraska they only don their Mayan clothing on special occasions.

The *traje* displays economic stability and cultural prowess for Mayan women, as they are not only costly, but also extremely time-consuming to make. Manuela details:

> The *huipiles* and *cortes* are very, very expensive, and can cost 500, 1500, or 2000 *quetzales* [the Guatemalan monetary unit, equivalent to $65, $195, or $260], depending on what the *traje* is like. Back in Guatemala each woman has about five *cortes* so they can change clothes every day. Some are simple, but the very beautiful ones are really expensive. In my family those that knew how weaved their *huipil,* blouse, and the *cinta,* sash to roll up in their hair. I can weave a little.
>
> When I came here I only brought the *traje* I was wearing while walking for about two days. You can't cross over with the *traje,* so we left them thrown out in the mountains when we crossed over the Mexican border, to change into clothes we brought. [She laughs nervously.] You get so *triiiiiste,* saaaad . . . because it's your *traje,* but that's it! You have to keep going. You have to keep walking. And then afterwards, here, you have to buy pants, a blouse, and a jacket.

After Manuela described the moment she parted with her *traje* we both fell silent for a long while.

With disappointment in her voice, Juana also explains this abandonment of Mayan clothing:

> When I came to the U.S. I wasn't wearing my *traje.* I was dressed like this, in American clothes, but there, I wear my *traje.* I didn't bring it with me when I crossed. They sent it to me afterwards. When you cross the border you don't bring anything. Nothing. Nothing at all.
>
> The *traje* I have here is for decoration. I don't wear it. Once when there was a Guatemalan *fiesta* here, a celebration, I did wear it. Oh my, when we have a *fiesta,* a celebration . . . it is so beauti-

ful. In Guatemala they have a lot of *fiestas* with a dance, and they are very, very beautiful.

The Mayan women must wear American clothes during the border crossing to hide their identity, from the time they set foot in Mexico. In that way, if intercepted and caught, they will only be sent as far south as they can convince border officials was their starting point.

María laments this drastic change of feigned identity that forces the abandonment of Mayan regional dress:

> In my village everyone was Mayan, and I used to wear my *traje* from my region. But I arrived here wearing these clothes, because if I had arrived wearing the *traje* they would know for sure that I'm from Guatemala. I left my *traje* in Guatemala, and when I go back to Guatemala, pretty soon, I will have to wear it. I don't have it here. It's that.... [Silence.] It's a big change for us. In the beginning, you feel bad because you are used to wearing your *traje,* your indigenous clothing, and here you wear other clothes. It's really awful. Some people who come here with a visa, come wearing the *traje* because they can travel here, to work, and then they go back, so they bring their *traje.* But we can't.

Donning American clothing is physically and emotionally estranging to the Mayan women. The physical loss of the *traje* takes place during the journey, but its emotional vestiges remain throughout the transition period into the new country, and these feelings still linger in their lives. Martha explains that in the end it is simply more cost effective to buy and wear out cheaper clothing, especially working in the meatpacking plant. Using the *traje* in the United States becomes secondary and superfluous. What they really need is money to support their children and to send home.

One time, when Martha spoke at a conference in California she donned a spectacular and gorgeously colorful *traje* bearing the Mayan calendar day symbols in bright turquoise, yellow, purple, red, and pink on a maroon background, with multicolored Guatemalan textile strips running the length. Together we admired it in silent awe, and Martha explained, "This is like any clothing. It goes in and out of style as the women change the patterns, colors, and designs, according to what occurs to them and the materials that are available. And the outfits themselves wear out. We like to have a lot of different *trajes.*" The presence and use of the day signs on this newer *traje* "reflect the reclamation of the Maya calendar . . . Like their ancestors before them, weavers design with purpose the universe into Maya cloth, creating continuity between the old and the new."[2]

Martha is adept at switching her dress here in the United States, in a place where the *traje* only holds one identifying meaning for unaware onlookers. In the past the women only wore the clothing from their village, but as transportation and communication improved, indigenous women gained access to *trajes* from different villages, and nowadays they don each other's clothes in an act of respect and appreciation, and also to economically support those who fashion and weave them by hand. In her book *La nieta de los mayas,* Rigoberta Menchú alludes to seeking out *trajes* to wear to give her acceptance speeches when she won the Nobel Peace Prize because there wasn't time to have a new one made. Word went out, and the women felt great joy and honor in offering the best *huipiles* they had from ceremonies, weddings, and celebrations to be worn for the Nobel acceptance ceremonies.[3] At times like this the Mayan indigenous female base is one and the same. Other times they joke about wearing the *traje* from another area, especially if they are planning on acting out at a dance or festival by having too much fun; the *traje* will confuse onlookers into thinking they are from the town it comes from, and in that way they avoid besmirching their own town's reputation, but this is said mostly in jest.

Most of the time the *traje* provokes admiration and respect, as their eyes light up when they talk about it. Mayan anthropologist Irma Alicia Velásquez Nimatuj explains the deep, intermeshed meaning beheld in the *traje* and its use for Mayan women: "Maya textiles and regional dress carry many meanings: cultural sym-

bolism, centuries of history, a changing and sometimes contra-
dictory indigenous culture, respect for nature, and so on. But it
is time to start recognizing that these same textiles also carry a
history of racial, cultural, social and economic exclusion that we
Maya of Guatemala have endured but have resisted for 479 years.
The textiles and regional dress are also a sign of the historical and
day-to-day resistance that Maya women have put up to maintain
and pass on their culture."[4]

Donning the *traje* and its relationship to identity and ethnic
origin has been a political issue for the women. Wearing the *traje*
was prohibited in Guatemala in schools using uniforms, but in
1999 education officials said indigenous students could attend
classes in their traditional dress rather than wearing a uniform.[5]
Again, the Mayan women have had to deal with discrimination
regarding their cultural attire on both sides of the border.

The Agreement on Identity and the Rights of Indigenous Peoples was signed in 1995, guaranteeing indigenous people the right
to wear their *traje*, and ensuring national respect for indigenous
clothing as well as intolerance for discrimination against those
wearing regional dress. In 2002 Velásquez Nimatuj was told she
couldn't enter a restaurant in Guatemala City because she was
wearing her *traje*. She describes the way the Guatemalan government's dependence on transnational capitalism, caused by new
political economic pressures linked to neoliberal changes in the
world economic system, has led to indigenous women's dress
being used to bolster the tourist industry: "Official state and economic elite policy at home and abroad has been to exploit Maya
people through the 'unequal exchange' of textiles that are bought
cheap from local Maya producers and sold at high prices to tourists, and to folklorize Maya cultures through cultural representations of Maya cultures that ignore the complex economic, social
and racial realities endured daily by some eight million Maya men
and women that live in this small Central American country."[6]
Similar to the Peace Accords, the agreements are in effect, but
the reality in the country remains largely unchanged.

The first time Martha's son, who was born in Nebraska, saw her wearing her *traje* at home, in preparation for a public presentation, he broke down in tears. "I was so concerned, and at the same time so hurt. I realized the core of my being is something entirely foreign, and even frightening to him. It was an awful moment of truth." The separation from home culture and identity felt by the migrating generation and the cultural reality as perceived by the younger generation in their new country are often at odds.

Manuela compares the low monthly wage she earned in Guatemala directly to the cost of a *traje*, demonstrating its priority for them. The indigenous dress and its accessibility become the symbol for identity, ethnicity, and favorable socioeconomic status or mobility. This direct relationship between employment earnings and *traje* purchasing power in the end determines that she cannot continue working in her country.

Having the *traje* stowed safely in Nebraska represents a part of all they left behind, and they attire themselves in it for celebrations, whereas in Guatemala their main concern has been sustenance, rather than whether they could wear the *traje*. They point out that wealthier indigenous Guatemalan women arrive in the United States by plane, wearing their *traje*, in a display that connotes the privilege of economic stability, but the poor are stripped of their identity in the desert. This constant shedding of identity, over and over, becomes "snake-like" in nature.

Ixchel is the Mayan goddess of weaving, childbearing, and healing. She is also the goddess of the moon, and women can relate to this, as both follow a twenty-eight-day cycle. She dons the two snakes that represent fatal venom as well as its healing power twisted together in a headdress that crowns her. Ixchel laid the groundwork for Mayan women to practice her legacy of adaptive behavior that always facilitates survival, as she empties out her vessel of old water in preparation for replenishing it with all things new, much in the same way that the women shed one country and clothing to take on a new one, or shed internalized oppression to revest themselves in the *traje* in Guatemala, as an act that frees them from the oppressor that had disrobed them of their cultural pride.

Kaqla, a Mayan women's group, has identified and deconstructed all these layers of shedding and adapting new attitudes regarding wearing their *traje* to ensure Mayan identity survives in a united front that is inclusive of the different ethnicities. They describe the shame that wearing the *traje* imbued due to racism, discrimination, and external attitudes that denigrated their culture. Dressing as Ladinos has also been portrayed as more professional, thus facilitating upward socioeconomic mobility, especially in the larger cities. When some Mayan women insisted their children wear indigenous dress to school, backed by the protection of the 1999 agreement, they were saddened when their children were victimized by both teachers and students. Mayans have participated in much thought and discussion regarding whether to continue using the *traje* or abandon its use.[7] Martha says: "When I am in or traveling to Guatemala I always wear my *traje maya*, Mayan dress, but here I don't. I would be really uncomfortable if I arrived there and I wasn't wearing my *traje*." This statement reflects how Martha deals with the struggles Mayan women have been through to assert their right to display self-identity and self-esteem. They wear the *traje* for "cultural and identity reasons, but also, as an important political and economic action, since it permits an economic movement related to weaving that provides earnings and economic autonomy to women."[8] For Martha, wearing her indigenous dress is a political, economic, and social activity, and as an indigenous activist, switching to Ladino dress would be an action denying her Q'anjob'al Mayan identity that she so prides.

Subsistence Farming, Sustenance, and Customs

Juana tells about a typical day as a child in Guatemala:

> In my village, when I was a little girl, my dad had lambs and sheep, and according to him, my sisters and I were there to do the work: "Go to work! Go gather the firewood." The women always have

to take the lambs out, at 9:00 or 10:00 a.m., and we don't come back home until 3:30 p.m. Every day! We would walk with them, but the lambs never want to go, or one gets away [giggles], and then they get into the corn and eat it, and then they show up at my dad's house without us, and when we get home he hits us and yells: "Go fetch the water!" "Wash the corn!" Well, it's really hard when your dad treats you badly and is really very overbearing and strict, yelling at you and hitting you with a belt. He hit us too much, but my mom didn't.

The women had to gather firewood for the wood-burning stoves or fire pits that are often located outdoors for cooking the tortillas and other food. They subsisted on what they grew, but often the crops were not plentiful enough to sustain their large families. According to *Report: Guatemala*, 50 percent of the population engage in some form of agriculture, often outside the monetized economy and at the subsistence level. The U.S. Environmental Protection Agency (EPA) states less than 1 percent of U.S. citizens currently engage in farming. These statistics demonstrate the discrepancy between subsistence and middle- and lower-class living between the two countries, as well as Americans' lesser participation in food production compared to Guatemalans.

Lucía details her family's experience farming, yet barely surviving:

In Guatemala the custom is we only eat beans, tortilla, and tamales. Now, thank God, my family there is a bit better off and has something to eat, even if it's just beans. We grow many varieties of beans and favas, and that's what we eat, all year. We also grow *milpa* [corn]. Even though my parents and all of us suffered, they were finally able to buy a little piece of land. We did it however we could, by not eating anything, or not having clothes at all. The only thing they taught us was to grow crops, and now they have their fields, and they are growing food right now, even though they are getting older, so they can eat.

María's situation as a Mayan female child in Guatemala was similar:

We indigenous women have been working since we were little girls! Now, my life here is very different from when I was a child. When I was five or six years old, they sent us, the girls, out to work, to bring water, to feed the animals, or to go to the mountain to look for wood. Sometimes our life wasn't like that, but usually we were working. The children here are so well taken care of, but there, at five or six years of age, they already have you washing your *traje*, sweeping . . . from the time you are a little girl you have to work.

Lucía further details her labor-intensive childhood duties and the extreme poverty as well: "I carried water to use in the house about twenty minutes each way, and I had to carry it, sometimes two containers, or return to bring more water. I carried one on my head and another big one in front of me in my arms, to get back faster." However, when she describes the bathing practice in preparation for the festive market days, a little reprieve from her childhood work is apparent:

In our village, to bathe, we have a place made out of adobe that's like a little house. In Mam we call it *chuj*. There's a little entry-way, and inside a little pile of stones for an oven. You start a fire with firewood, and put a bucket of water on it. You sweat in there because it's really hot, and there are some wood boards lined up, and you can cut some *zacate*, or hay, some *sauco*, or *chilca*, it's a plant, and you go inside, lie down on those boards, and you always take a pitcher of water in with you, and you throw water over the coals of the fire. You rub the *sauco* on your body so it will clean you and heat your body up. That's the custom for bathing that we have there, but here we don't do that, but I would like to. We do it from the time we are babies, and we even put that plant on the babies. It's a *limpieza*, a cleansing. Each person decides when their body is good and hot, and you bring a container of water and soap and you wash up. For me it's so relaxing, with the vapor and the flames of the fire. You feel so very good. It even takes away the pain in your body. If you have a backache, you tap yourself with the plant where it hurts, and the next day it doesn't hurt! Over there we do that two or three times a week. In the village where we live, everyone goes in, on Wednesdays and Saturdays, to get all cleaned up for the market, so you can go there nice and clean.

And on Sunday, it's market day! Everyone goes, but we walk for an hour and a half to get to the plaza where the market is because we don't have money to pay for the truck. At the market it's really lively with lots of people in the streets. They put stands with oranges, bananas, mangoes . . . there are a lot of things for sale! There is a part of the market with herbs like *nabo*, turnip greens, and *mostaza*, mustard greens, and we buy herbs. There is also *hierba mora*, mint, which I've seen here, and I grow it here when it's the season. In Guatemala we go to the river to look for *berros*, watercress, and they even sell that in a store here in this city. I like it! It's so delicious. We look for greens to eat because we're poor.

And the pervasive poverty resurfaces as Lucía details how they are forced to seek out the food growing wild in the countryside to subsist, and now, she actively seeks out native Guatemalan foods here.

All the women are deeply concerned about providing nutritional meals for their children as they conscientiously learn about the new foods. Juana is especially attentive to her children's nutritional needs:

I want to stay here, and fight for my children. My four-year-old daughter won't eat tortilla, but back there, in Guatemala there isn't any other food, just tortilla. We eat them with vegetables they call *hierba*, herbs and greens, with beans, or *chile*, hot peppers. We don't eat just tortilla alone, it's always with something else, such as *atol*, a drink made from corn flour, but there isn't as much meat and potatoes as here. I prefer the food there because it doesn't have as much fat, but on the other hand, here, I don't know how to prepare it, because the *hierbas*, herbs and greens that we eat here, aren't the same as the ones in Guatemala. We eat cabbage, turnip greens, and watercress too. *Apazote* is like cilantro, it gives the food flavor so we put it with chicken or beans. There are so many types of *hierbas*, herbs and greens, in Guatemala.

Martha explains how difficult life was for the Mayan indigenous women raised in poor families, and how this sways their decision to stay or return home:

I have spoken with many women, asking them if they want to go back to Guatemala, and they say no, no way on earth do they want to go back because they had to wash the clothes in the river, and the water was cold, and they had to prepare the food for their father-in-law, they had to gather firewood, cut the wood and it was damp so it was hard to start the fire. They had to make the tortillas by hand because the men don't like to eat the ones from the store. You have to boil the corn, shell the corn, and grind it; it's easier to buy the tortillas. I have spoken with lots of women that don't want to return. Life is harder. You have to get up early to go work. The situation for women is more difficult over there. Here you work hard, but it's eight hours and you start off working at minimum wage. It must be hard at the meatpacking plant. Sometimes the meat is frozen, with a huge piece connected to the bone, and it's the same job every day. Some of them were living and working here, and their hands ended up arthritic.

According to Martha, in indigenous families the Mayans think it is the female's job to work and serve the males, and that is the reason they don't "produce them economically," meaning that they don't invest in women's education or professional training like they do for men. In this way children have been seen as commodities, as a moving part of the labor machine that will keep the family subsisting and surviving. Each member must be invested in and maintained according to their socioeconomic function in the family and culture, following Mayan family dynamics of poverty and gender inequity.

Menchú outlines the same: "As a rule, we girls don't play, because our mothers find it hard to let a girl go off and play on her own. Girls have to learn to look after things in the home, they must learn all the little things their mothers do. Mothers never sit around at home with nothing to do. They're always busy. If they haven't any specific job to do, they've always got their weaving, and if they haven't any weaving, there's always something else. So our games are mostly weaving or things like that, but at least we can do it together."[9] Once the women have experienced life in the United States, working, but with modern conveniences, few want to return.

Transnational Families

The Mayan women's main concern is family, both immediate and extended; it lies at the center of their lives. Their family sizes in Guatemala varied from eight to eleven members. Juana tells about her situation:

> I'm from a big family with five sons and four daughters, but my husband only has his mom and dad. I have three brothers here in this city, and three in Guatemala that I send money to every month, for my two daughters that are twelve and nine years old. Here I have a daughter that's four years old, and my baby son is three weeks old. I am so crazy. I got married when I was still a little girl, only 14 years old. In Guatemala that's normal. My parents didn't want me to get married, and I am still married to him. We got together there, and then he came here first, and I stayed with the two girls there. Later, he sent me the money for my trip, and then I came. I left my daughters with my dad, because my mom already died, of an illness.

At this point in the interview, Juana wanted to know about my life as well, inquiring if I had children. I explained that here some women decide if they want to have children or not, and asked whether it was the same for the Mayan women. Laughing, she replied: "Here, yes, sometimes, we decide, but back home in Guatemala we don't, because God knows and tells us how many children we will have after we get married. Here some of the women have surgery to not have children, and the husband doesn't mind because they already have children. Now, I don't want to have more children, but I think I'm going to have some. I am trying now, not to have more. It's different how they do that here."

Religious beliefs and gender inequities have determined these women's reproduction practices, but once they relocate, are employed, and acquire relative economic stability in their new home, they begin questioning and reshaping traditional Mayan practices. Juana doesn't seem to be aware of birth control methods; the only option she knows about is an operation. As well, her description of men's attitudes toward women who have hysterectomies after bearing children reflects how women's bodies provide the offspring that physically manifest their masculinity. In *machista,* or male chauvinist society, men sometimes reject and divorce infertile women or women who only have female offspring, and during the armed conflict many Mayan women who suffered repeated rapes were abandoned by their husbands. Juana also asks me what women do when they're old and don't have children to take care of them, pointing out the intergenerational familial expectations of support among Mayans.

One of the Mayan women confided to me that when her husband insisted they continue having children and she was of a different mind, he said they should go talk to the Catholic priest. She explained to him that she didn't want the priest to decide what she should or shouldn't do with her body, exerting her womanly right to control what happens within her personal realm. Again, immigrating opens new dimensions of living to the Mayan women.

Labor

Most of the Mayan women detail the widespread poverty that forced them to work as children. Finding lucrative employment unavailable in the villages, some sought out opportunities in nearby cities in an effort to assist their parents and find a way to prosper more. After giving birth to her first son, Lucía left her village to work as a live-in domestic servant in a nearby city to support him. She tells about this experience:

> I went to work in the capital, in Guatemala, for about three years, and then, after that, I was working in Quetzaltenango too, as a domestic servant in private homes. It didn't go very well for me. In Guatemala I suffered a lot, because the *señora*, the woman of the house, was really strict and rebellious in her house, sometimes even fighting with her own daughter about me when she pointed out she was treating me like a slave. That was because I used to go to bed at 1:00 in the morning, and I had to get up at 3:00 or 4:00 in the morning. [Shouting,] I slept for two hours in that house! And I had to clean, and nothing could be left undone. The *señora* would come home, and she would run her fingers over the sofa, the VCR, the television, the stereo, the door, to see if it had dust. [In a louder voice,] Ay, oh my, how I suffered. I even had to wash the clothes by hand. There were so many clothes! There were about seven people in the house! [Two little children come out of a closed bedroom and the whole mood changes, becoming much softer.] The truth is, I have two children there and two here. So many things have happened to us already. I suffered a lot, and I didn't sleep much, and I would get really tired, because I washed the clothes at four in the morning, at five in the morning the *señora* left for work and I had to squeeze two dozen oranges with the juicer and leave the juice in the refrigerator every morning, and they would stop to serve themselves their juice and then they would go to work. Yes, it was very early. I had to wash, clean, *trapear*, mop, squeeze the juice, and have the floor shiny. I shined, shined, and shined. The daughter asked the mother, "Why are you trying to kill her with so much work? She is tired. Poor thing. She is here out of need. She is working out of need. It's a struggle for her to get ahead in her life!" And her mom yelled, "What do you

have to do with this? That woman has to do what I tell her to do in my house! I want to have my clothes ironed!" I ironed until one in the morning to finish all the clothes. And one day I said to her, "*Señora,* I can't do it anymore. I am going to leave. I am going to go work for another *señora.*" I worked seven days a week at that job.

Poverty and single motherhood forced Lucía to work as a domestic servant in a difficult situation, until it became unbearable. However, after suffering abuse, moving from town to town to change employers, and realizing the wage was too low, she ended up back in her village, returning to her in-law's home with her husband. She tells:

After working in two cities and returning to my village, I went home again to live with my husband because there the whole family lives together in one house. The girls always go to live with the in-laws. However, it never went well with my mother-in-law. The woman treated me very badly, telling me I wasn't the type of daughter-in-law she wanted. I told her, "Well, that's fine, but the truth is your son loves me." And then, later, since he was a big womanizer and had a lot of women, he would go with one, and then another, and another, and so I separated from him. Now some Mayan women sometimes get separated if the men mistreat them, or if they do whatever they want. I went to work in Quetzaltenango, pregnant with the other baby. I had a son, and I cleaned the house, and they used to give me extra money and the key so I could come and go whenever I wanted. I used to go for walks with my son in the park a lot. I was very happy. Thank God it went so well for me.

Lucía suffered abuse as an employee, a daughter-in-law, and wife, but later found refuge in a respectful work situation.

Gender, Education, and Language

In our group meetings the women voiced their concern about the internalization of cultural practices that entrap women as servants for men. They wondered aloud if this was the cause of the low self-esteem they often felt, having had to serve the men and receive less schooling than them. Juana tells of the gender discrimination and favoritism in Mayan families that has left the women feeling inferior to their male counterparts in the family unit:

In Guatemala, the parents always love the boys more than the girls. When a boy is born they buy clothes, shoes, and everything. They also take good care of them, or they treat them well, and they hardly do that with the girls. They love the girls too, my mom and dad love me, but not the way they love the boys. That's just how it is. They love them more because they are men, and they know they are going to stay and live with the parents. The daughter-in-law is going to come live in their house, and they like that. He's not going to leave, but the women are going to go with the men. They are not going to stay at home.

In Guatemala I lived in a village, in Santa Eulalia, so I speak Q'anjob'al. But here in Nebraska, at my house, we speak English only!! [Seeing how she has shocked me, she then bursts out into hearty laughter.] No, it's not true! At home we speak Q'anjob'al only. That's why . . . I don't speak Spanish well. I just speak a little bit. It's difficult for me. In Q'anjob'al it's not hard to speak, I know how to talk and I can say whatever I want. But in Spanish, I practically can't, because when we were little, living with my mom and my dad, we only spoke Q'anjob'al, so we didn't know Spanish. I only learned a little in Guatemala at school because I only went for three years. When your parents have money you can go to school, and the men get to go to school because they love them. I noticed my older brother was in school for about five years, and my other brother for six years, but my two sisters and sister-in-law didn't go to school at all. I liked school, but three years wasn't long enough. I had eight brothers and sisters, and I had a lot of homework, but I didn't do it, and then my dad would get angry. Sometimes when you are little, you don't know what you are doing. My notebook was a mess. My dad scolded and hit me, saying, "You have to learn." It wasn't a good experience for me at all, but thank God, I can write the letters, my name and address, and read, all in Spanish, but in Q'anjob'al, I practically can't, but those of us who have studied, can.

Many of the women lamented what they suffered when they arrived not speaking Spanish or English. According to Lucía, "There are more Guatemalans in Nebraska that don't speak Spanish than there are that do." However, she didn't personally suffer the language barrier the same way Juana did:

I already knew Spanish when I arrived here, and my Mayan language is Mam. At home, back in Guatemala, we only spoke Mam. I went to school and there the teachers only speak Spanish, they don't speak Mayan languages, and that's where I first started learning Spanish. It was a little hard for me to learn, and it was difficult when I started school and couldn't speak Spanish, but then you just start learning the way they write the letters that they give to you and you start learning. The truth is I studied two or three years in school. In Guatemala, a lot of children cannot go to school because they have to work with their family.

José, the Ladino male, was more fortunate in his educational experience. He studied well and even attended college:

I am not Mayan. I am of the Ladino race, and I don't speak any Mayan language, only Spanish. It's normal for a Ladino to go to the university because everyone that can afford it goes. My parents made a huge sacrifice and I was able to study, and I managed to graduate with an elementary teaching degree. After that I was only able to continue studying towards my undergraduate degree at the university for one more year, because I was already married by the time I went.

María also finished her elementary schooling and studied at the university level as well:

In Guatemala I studied, but I have fewer studies than Martha. I finished my degree as a certified accountant in Guatemala, and I worked three months in that field. Since my dad doesn't have much money, he could only help each of us study for six years, and after that he advised me to study and work so I would have a little money. I moved to another town and I went back to see my parents each year. I worked during the day and studied at night. That's how I finished secondary school, and I decided to finish my studies and graduate. When I was almost finished, with only two more years to go, and with that I would earn enough money to eat, the company boss gave me a different post, and little by little I moved up, working five years in that company, in Guatemala City.

As María stated, she is well aware that Martha is the most educated in their immediate circle in the meatpacking city. In Martha's family, education was highly respected and valued; it is a gift she has appreciated, and in her interview she effectively analyzed the system and cultural practices surrounding education. She explains how she studied and managed to complete a university degree:

> My parents taught me Spanish and Q'anjob'al, my native language. My paternal grandmother taught all her children to read and write, and she was the one who insisted on education. They would read the Bible because back then there weren't teachers. The people who knew how to read and write taught everyone else, and later in life, that is what helped them get a more stable job. The priest in the village asked one of them to teach classes to the children in the parish school, and another worked in the health center, and my grandfather was a carpenter and catechist. My dad told me that in the past, if you just knew how to read and write, you could be a teacher. Later, they hired the people who had completed sixth grade in primary school to be teachers, and when they saw that there were others that kept studying

and graduated as teachers, they were the ones that were given the first opportunity to work. My dad told me it's good to continue studying, because the time is going to come when a university degree is going to be obligatory.

My parents attended the parish school that the Maryknoll priests founded. This school has helped a lot of indigenous people study. In my class, out of the fifty-four students in sixth grade, thirteen were girls. The girls that live in the small villages do not go to school because of the distance away from their homes. People think that a woman's job is to take care of the children, and do the housework, such as the cooking and washing, but that has now changed in my village. There are more professional women that work as teachers, and many of the young boys no longer finish their studies because they want to go to the U.S.

Education is important. Sometimes some teachers tried to talk down to us, using easy words so that we could understand them, because Spanish wasn't our first language. But when I changed boarding schools, the teachers spoke to us with more difficult words, even though we were indigenous. They said that we had to learn the different terminologies because we were going to need them when we became teachers in our villages, and that motivated me even more. They said not only were we going to become teachers in our own villages, but that we also had to reach out even deeper into the community to make a difference and motivate more parents to send their daughters to school. They taught us that being indigenous doesn't mean that one has to learn only one thing.

In Guatemala there were scholarships from the U.S. I took the exams to apply, and then the university paid for my studies. Only seven people won those scholarships. After that I continued on to become a teacher, which was three years of study, with a practicum, and I graduated with a teaching degree, but I kept studying at the university, and I graduated in psychology. The Q'anjob'al Mayan women take the lead in graduating with an undergraduate degree, and my village has also had a Q'anjob'al woman for mayor.

I used to travel to Quetzaltenango on the weekends to study at the university, and from Monday to Friday I worked in my village teaching classes to primary school children, and in the afternoon, in a secondary school. Some people in the town looked down on the fact that I was traveling alone because it's not common to see a young woman traveling alone at 1:00 or 2:00 in the morning. The normal or customary thing is to see young boys or men traveling because they are merchants or businessmen, but a woman? A woman should be at home. Their accusatory looks said more than any words could.

Martha points out the Mayan expectation that those with knowledge share it with others to enhance the social and intellectual standing of all indigenous people, an attitude stressed in Menchú's work as well.[10] María also practiced this: "I remember when I learned to write Q'anjob'al. I paid for the classes in a private business for a year because they only teach Spanish in school. After that I worked a year in my village teaching the people who don't know how to read and write, in their two languages at once. Here in Nebraska there are women that don't know how to read and write, and it makes it really hard for them." This explains the disturbing fact that at the end of our group meetings they always asked, "Anna, can't you stay here and teach us English?"

In our interviews the Mayan women have pointed out and lamented the lowered gender expectations and benefits for women in their society, detailing the limitations they faced in their families, culture, country, and economic situation. The criticism Martha suffered while teaching and studying at the university is common. The girls in her class had to travel from hamlets or villages to attend schools in larger cities, and the physical distance from urban centers is an added economic deterrent, with gender-oriented restraints because girls aren't allowed to leave home alone. Menchú also explains these cultural practices that limit Mayan women: "When there are fiestas, even a village fiesta, girls mustn't leave their mother's side. Even in our own village we have to stay with our mother, so that people will respect girls who are growing up. Our parents say that a girl who goes off on her own learns bad things and becomes a girl who hangs about the streets. She must stay with her parents. So in the fiestas, although we say hello to the others and so on, we always stay by our mother's side."[11]

Unlike some Mayan women in her community and country, Martha has been taught to cross and move beyond these gender barriers, to pursue her educational and professional skills and intelligence. Her higher education and persistent professional activity automatically elevate her into a female role model that some oppressed women cannot apparently support because her behavior lies outside of the cultural norm.

Poverty

The lack of access to education is rooted in gender inequity, but is also exacerbated by extreme poverty and the need for child labor in the family. Lucía names poverty as the driving force leading the Guatemalan Mayans to Nebraska:

> There are a lot of Guatemalans here, but in reality, they arrive all the way to this country looking for something out of necessity. One really suffers in Guatemala because there is a lot of poverty. It's hard, because there you earn money, but not like here, where you earn a little better, so you can then send it over there. Some people have houses with roofs, that have tiles already, but they aren't any good, they don't serve their purpose anymore, because they have rust already. They're old. You survive, but in Guatemala I suffered a lot of poverty in my home. My mom had nine children, but because of poverty we didn't have money to pay for medicine, and FIVE, FIVE of her children died! [Silence.]

Her oldest sister is in Guatemala; Lucía is the second child. The brother that followed her died because her father couldn't afford the medicine prescribed for the sores all over his body, so he just gave him smaller doses. Her father had to live with the remorse that he hadn't been able to give everything to his son. Three sisters and another brother were born and died, and her younger sister survived and lives in Guatemala. She laments the poverty that did not allow adequate health care, thus taking her siblings' lives:

We had a house, but the truth is the roof was of straw, it wasn't tile, and that was the only thing we had. Poverty. And my dad was going to work with people, and we were helping, growing potatoes, sowing *milpas*, hoeing, clearing the ground . . . we watched others throw the seeds on the ground and that's what we did. We earned our money, and we helped him with the expenses at home, but it wasn't enough for all the medicine. And after that, my other brother that I have here was born and he's seventeen years old now. I arrived before him, and I brought him here to this country, but, the truth is, we still live in poverty, we still haven't gotten out of it. It's okay, that's just the way it is. We are still working on that. Now we are trying to help my family however we can, to give something to them, and, to help them, so they can have something. I had my first son, but he is in Guatemala, and he is ten years old now. Here we are paying rent on this house, but in Guatemala we have a little house made of adobe.

I saw how my father suffered for us. He set a good example for us, and now, we will suffer for a time. It really hurt me too, when my sisters and brothers died. There was so much sadness. My mother just fell apart thinking, "Because I am a poor person, I don't have money, I don't have anything, and that's the reason why my children died." My mom was destroyed for about a year, thinking that maybe she was the one who killed her children. We, the oldest ones, gave her advice, telling her she shouldn't blame herself, that God knows that it wasn't our fault, that we did everything we could for them. But they died anyway. My mom always used to get started and do some things around the house, but then, when she'd remember, she'd start crying about all this. A lot of things happen to us in our life.

Poverty has held a firm grip on some of the Mayan women since they were children, and as Lucía states, they are still struggling to get out of it. Being denied education and having to work from the time they were children has created a strong survival mechanism in all of the women. Lucía reiterates that poverty has been the main issue her entire life:

When I was a girl I noticed how we lived in and suffered such poverty, and when I got older, I wanted to help my dad. My sister and I gave them money, and that's when they got a little better and they started to build a house. They built it, and we were helping with the expenses, such as buying tiles for the roof.

When we came home from working we would make a chili pepper with potatoes, and it would last us two days. That's how we eat; whatever we can due to the poverty that is so difficult in Guatemala. Sometimes, we had nothing more than one egg, and we would make a broth, with just one egg, and we shared it amongst all of us. My grandparents, my mom, my dad, and we four children were there, and one egg amongst all of us was all we had! They put a little sprig of *apazote*, cilantro in with the egg, but what they are giving you is really just water in a pot, and you have to share it amongst yourselves. That is what happened to us.

We spent a lot of years like that, until we came here. And as a little girl, sometimes you cry because . . . the truth is, I have cried from the time I started school. I used to wear a *corte*, skirt, and it was missing a panel, a little piece. [She holds up her fingers to indicate the four inches of fabric that were missing to cover her hip and leg.] It was missing, and I couldn't . . . I would bend down, to pick something up, and then my skirt would open up, and we didn't have money to buy a new *corte* for me. Since we are poor, we have to buy them, because sometimes you don't know how to weave. My sister started to weave, at a class, because it's cheaper if you make it. At my house we only weaved aprons, belts . . . that's all we made because, there wasn't anything, and when we went to buy the materials it was too expensive. And the blouse I wore had a tear. It was really, really ugly. Once I got older, when I started working, I started buying my clothes.

Manuela grew up in an impoverished family as well:

Yes, I'm poor. That's just how it is. When I was born, as a little girl, since there were seven of us, five girls and two boys, my dad was so very poor. There wasn't enough money for clothes or for food because there were too many of us. We are poor. That's why, I decided to leave. "It's better if I go. I'm going to work in the capital," I told them. I worked for three months in the capital, cleaning, changing beds, doing everything for 300 *quetzales* [$38] a month. I was earning so little a month that the money wouldn't cover the expenses, and to buy a *traje*, it costs about 200 to 300 *quetzales* [$25–$38]. That's what it's worth. Clothes are cheap here, you can buy pants and a jacket, but there clothing is really expensive.

Here they quickly see the consumer accessibility of basic needs such as food and clothing, and they try to send part of their newly achieved income back home via mail. Those that are documented travel back and forth, and they take advantage of their trips to physically transport consumer goods with them. Martha details the economic incongruence:

I have been back to Guatemala twice. When I go back, I would like the modern conveniences I have here in my house to also be there. What I like the most is the ease with which people can buy something if they want it. In Guatemala, it's more expensive. You receive less for what you pay for. One day I do want to return because I didn't live through a lot of poverty, but the other Mayan women say, "And me? What am I going to do at home? I would like to have a job." Here there are more modern conveniences. I have a car, I can work, I can go to school. We have lots of independence. And people like to buy things. Over there, they can't, because there isn't enough money. There, it's a luxury to go to

Burger King or McDonald's. A peasant can't go. But here, everyone can go. Over there, everything is more expensive.

The Mayan families in both the United States and Guatemala
constantly struggle to achieve greater economic security. María
reiterates the contrast in poverty levels:

Maybe they do suffer here, but it's less than we do. It might be
like what I've heard about California, that the Americans that
are poor always have a car or have a house or something. However, in Guatemala, the people that are poor don't have money
or anything. We are the ones that are really poor. For example,
in Ohio I know some Americans that are poor. They don't have
money, but they are richer than the people who say they are rich
in Guatemala. They have a car, a house, and their garage. Americans are not bad, but I think they can't see reality. I think when
a person finally gets something, they aren't satisfied. They always
want something more.

María pinpoints the economic disparity between citizens from
each country. According to World Bank data for 2012, 54 percent
of the population in Guatemala lived below the poverty level, with
a per capita income of $3,140 versus $50,120 in the United States.
The National Poverty Center states 15.1 percent lived in poverty
in the United States in 2010.

María understands that the impact of being "poor" varies across
borders. Her father has the same desire for a higher income as
Americans. He will even encourage sibling rivalry in an effort to
increase the familial income, and thus acquire more consumer
goods:

One day my dad told my brothers and sisters that he loved me
more than them because I gave him more money, and I told him,
"You don't have any reason to love me more because I give you
more money," and my dad says to me, "Daughter, you are the
only one who is helping me. You help me more than your brothers and sisters." But then they felt bad. I would give him money,

and two sisters gave him money too, and he said to me, "It's that I don't have money. I want to buy myself things and I don't have money." I knew that I gave him a lot because I had studied, and my sisters were unhappy, so I gave a little to my dad and a little to my sisters, so that nobody would feel bad. My dad said to me, "If you are earning more money, it's because you put in more effort."

When comparing U.S. and Guatemalan family incomes it becomes apparent that one solution for much of the growing immigration rates would have been improved economic development in countries such as Guatemala. According to the International Organization for Migration, IOM, limited economic opportunities and the lack of access to formal education, social services, and credit are the main causes for emigration. International free trade policies such as the North American Free Trade Agreement, NAFTA, implemented in 1994 by the United States, Canada, and Mexico, expanded in 2004 to five Central American countries through the Central America Free Trade Agreement (CAFTA), and extended to include the Dominican Republic in 2006, were intended to stimulate economic trading levels with these countries. Improving weak and flailing economies would have kept these residents in their own countries, but a long history of colonization by European nations, and more recently, economic and political forays by the United States, have negatively affected less developed countries such as Guatemala.

People abroad often indicate they do not want to leave home or their children. Unemployment and a growing family led José and many to leave. He states: "After I graduated from the university, when I couldn't find a job, I found myself forced to try and get a job in the army." Like so many of his educated peers during the time of the armed conflict, José sadly realized his best option for working and supporting his wife and two children was joining the military. He experienced the civil war directly, serving as an active soldier in his community and the surrounding areas. The Mayan women we interviewed—if they didn't witness the massacres that took place in neighboring communities and in the center of the country—recalled the conflict in a fragmented and childlike manner because they were mere children at the time. Juana speaks of her village with great affection, and she encourages me to visit it, but she also remembers the underlying danger in her community caused during the civil war when suspected *guerrilleros*, or guerrilla insurgency fighters, came into town and the *patrulleros*, the civil patrol officers, obligatorily organized and overseen by the army, joined forces to drive them out.

I remember Huehuetenango all the time, and I remember some things about the war in my village, because the soldiers did come. My dad was working with the *patrulleros*, in a group, and they would go looking for someone. I was a little girl, and I don't remember well, but one time they shouted out, and they were all running, but they couldn't follow him, and the two *guerrilleros* were carrying guns. My dad was at home, doing his work, but then all the people started following the *guerrilleros* and when they found them they ran into the mountains, where there's a lot of forest, in the jungle. We were searching and searching, and later, with horses, but they didn't find them. The *guerrilleros* are really bad, really violent.

Another time a man in the village was suspected of being a *guerrillero*. They followed him, so he left, he ran, and then everyone jumped into the water shouting, "There he is," and they threw a rock in the water, aiming at him. When my brother and dad arrived, the *guerrilleros* wanted to kill my dad, and a bullet hit his horse, but it didn't die. The patrollers take care of people or families because sometimes the *guerrilleros* arrive. Sometimes there are patrollers from other villages. Now, near my house, I don't know, but I don't think there's any violence anymore. Now, there are thieves, that's all.

In the towns the local patrol groups worked diligently to expel anyone suspected of collaborating with the *guerrilla* because often their presence attracted military intervention. Juana sensed the severity of the situation although she didn't understand it fully as a child. Martha tells what it was like in her town, reiterating that because she lived in the business center of the western highlands, they fortunately did not experience the most violent atrocities other communities did:

> Compared to other municipalities in Huehuetenango, my town was affected by the armed conflict, but to a lesser degree. It may be because the majority of its inhabitants are merchants and business people that did business with nearby municipalities, and with Mexico while the army was pursuing the *guerrilla* in other municipalities. In San Miguel Acatán and in San Mateo Ixtatán there were a lot of massacres. I remember those things from when I was a little girl. I remember the bombs, that the earth would shake, but I thought it was lightning striking, or an earthquake. So, during the time of the armed conflict, I really wasn't affected.

The civil war dragged on for more than thirty years, but for the Mayan women now in Nebraska it was largely in the distance. However, José experienced it firsthand in the military. The following chapter discusses the civil war that drove increased emigration to the United States. It narrates José's experience serving in the Guatemalan army, as well as Martha's work as an indigenous Mayan woman serving on the Peace Commissions after the Peace Accords.

2

Guatemalan Civil War and Postwar Rebuilding

From 1954 to 1996 Guatemala suffered a civil war largely backed by the United States because of its economic interests there. After World War II, the United States maintained a good relationship with Guatemalan presidents such as freely elected Jorge Ubico, in office from 1931 to 1944, in order to keep contact with the American corporation, the United Fruit Company, and its affiliate, International Railways of Central America. These companies were the country's two largest employers, a fact underlying the Guatemalan leaders' need to accommodate them, and landless Mayans were laborers on the government projects these companies conducted.[1]

From 1944 to 1954 the country was ruled first by Juan José Arévalo, and then his disciple Jacobo Arbenz. However, when Arbenz began redistributing land to the poor, President Eisenhower, CIA director Allen Welsh Dulles, and Secretary of State John Foster Dulles organized Operation Success, overthrowing Arbenz, and putting U.S. Army–trained Carlos Castillo Armas in power. At the time Allen Dulles was on the board of directors of the United Fruit Company. From 1954 to 1996 a military junta ruled the country. In 1960 organized guerrilla activity modeled after that in Fidel Castro's Cuba surged forth from the highlands to combat the military, leaving the poor, rural, and indigenous populations caught in the cross fire between the two forces. In 1970 President Carlos Arana Osorio began assassinating or "disappearing"[2] anyone suspected of sympathizing with the insurgents. This was followed by the scorched earth campaign from 1977 to

1982 under president and general Efraín Ríos Montt in which villages suspected of helping the *guerrilla* were annihilated. In 1982, the various guerrilla forces regrouped, causing even more confusion among civilians, who could no longer identify allegiances or affiliations. Chaos and genocide ensued as civilian populations suspected of collaborating with the *guerrilla* were decimated by the military. Often both civilians and former guerrilla members who had later joined military forces attacked *guerrilleros* in the communities, resulting in clouded allegiances and widespread confusion. During the more than thirty-six year conflict, there were over 200,000 deaths, and a million civilians were displaced. Some of them, including our interviewees, ended up in Nebraska.

I met Martha, some of the other Mayan women, and José—a former Guatemalan army soldier—at a Catholic church in Nebraska. Quiet and humble Latinos gathered there, and eventually it was standing room only. I had notified the priest of my research interests, so that he could inform the congregation and facilitate my conversations with the Mayan women. However, when he introduced me, and turned the pulpit over to me without warning, I was overcome by fear. Passing before the eyes of the crowd, I fumbled my way to the front of the church, faced the congregation, and began speaking to them in Spanish. For the first time since I had moved back I didn't feel like I was actually in Nebraska at all; it was more like I was in Santiago Atitlán, Santa Cantarina Palopó, Chichicastenango, Huehuetenango, Quetzaltenango, or Chiapas. As is customary among people from this culture, I was treated with utmost respect and attention. Suddenly no one was moving or talking. I explained I was a *profesora*, instructor in a college for the *comunidad*, community, and that I was researching Guatemalan Mayan women authors and wanted to hear about Mayan women's experience in the United States. I explained my belief that it is only through dialogue that we can understand one another better. After a split second of silence, the entire congregation broke into applause, which shamed and shocked me. I scurried back to my pew.

Then the father's lay assistant, José, gathered the women, encouraging them to come near me. They looked somewhat leery and suspect. They were being singled out yet once again, and what for this time? I stood up to welcome them over to me, but once they were closer I quickly sat down again because I physically loomed over them. I showed them the poems from the Mayan women authors I had studied, and offered them copies. They seemed perplexed by me, by my papers, by this sudden interest in them and in Mayan women. However, they were kind and compliant, and graciously gave me their phone numbers. I thought to myself, that day and many days afterward, that if I had been them, I don't know if I would have handed over my phone number. Although I had only requested to talk to the women, José lingered too near the group. He waited until I had spoken to the women individually. He seemed to understand the women's need. Finally he approached me and in a near whisper he told me part of his story, and I benefited greatly from his patience and candor.

José: A Soldier in the Army

José's story mirrors that of many Guatemalan and other young men and women who join the armed forces because there is always work there. He is the only male included in this book about Guatemalan Mayan women living around and working in the meatpacking plants of eastern Nebraska. He provides an additional dimension to this project: how individuals seeking success are drawn toward military service. José shares:

> Years ago, after I graduated from the university, when I couldn't find a job, I found myself forced to try and get a job in the army. Getting into the army back then was very easy because the armed conflict had already started. However, to get out, was extremely difficult because anyone that was a member of the army was at risk and had to be under the army's control. And anyone who had never been in the army was at risk with the *guerrilla* of Guatemala. Therefore, it was a really difficult state of affairs. Even within the

army, I suffered so many things. I carry all that very deep inside, and I think I am never going to forget all those traumas and illnesses. There are things that will remain marked within me for the rest of my life.

I was in the army for seven years, and there was a lot of armed conflict between the army and the *guerrilla*. On numerous occasions the *guerrilla* attacked the military zone where I was in the early morning hours or late at night. You no longer lived in peace. You were sleeping, but always wondering what time they would come to attack, and the *guerrilla* and the army no longer measured the consequences. The army fired shots to the outside and the *guerrilla* fired shots inside the military compound, but they didn't factor in the consequences of the fact that on the outside there were civil communities.

These were really difficult moments, and, to a certain degree, a human being is not prepared for all that. After so much attack, attack, attack, it begins to build up a trauma, and in the long run it affects a person psychologically. And that's how, after living through so many things, there came a time that I sunk down into a really difficult period. I got sick on various occasions, the last time while doing physical training, when I fell down in the sports compound of the military base, and I hit my head, and after that my nervous system started failing. That, on top of the trauma I already had in my system, affected me way too much. I had to go to professionals to ask for help because I was feeling really bad. To a certain degree I thought I was losing my mind, because of all of the trauma, and because of everything that had happened, and everything I saw inside the military base, which included many human rights violations. Many of the people who were providing obligatory military service were our people from the rural areas, the peasant people, the poorest people in Guatemala, and they had to put up with all of it, to the point of maybe even losing their lives.[3] Inside the military zone, many things happened. The military officials beat the soldiers and tortured.

Possibly, due to the type of discipline that defines institutions like the military, human beings abuse. However, within the same armed institution I met really good people, higher ups that were really noble, with really good emotions, and I also hold them in my memory, and I don't forget them because they were really good, high quality people. I would say about 7 percent of the people in the armed institution are of very human quality. The rest are really bad. They committed really severe punishments at midnight, in the early dawn, and they hit and jailed soldiers for things that didn't even matter.

What they did the most was make you drink salt water, and then you lose control of your bodily functions. It all goes to water. Then they wanted you to keep doing your exercises. And a human being weakens. A human being can't take all of this. They would overcome you with blows from the butt of their guns, or by kicking you, or they would take a machete and with the smooth side of it they would hit you wherever it landed on your back. There were really severe punishments, such as when they would hang you from the bed, with your arms tied to the head of the bed and your body naked, like Christ, with your feet hanging in the air, and they blindfolded your eyes, and tied all your limbs, and started hitting you in the stomach. And if you fell down, they would start the same all over again, and you had to put up with it, never knowing at what time of the night they would come to punish you because your eyes were blindfolded. There were really difficult situations that many suffered through.

As a result of all this I suffered a blow to the stomach, and I was in horrible pain during eight days until I vomited blood while doing night duty. I felt like my stomach was huge, and all wounded inside. I would try to eat, but I felt discomfort in my body. They took me to a hospital, and then they transferred me to the capital as an emergency, traveling five hours by car to get there. They started treating me, they ran tests on my stomach, and they discovered an ulcer had formed where the wound hadn't healed so I was under treatment for a number of years. What happened is my wound ulcerated, and due to the stress I was living in, the ulcer could not close, because after that it became a nervous ulcer, and the situation that I was in, that caused the ulcer, was also provoking stomach problems. It took a long time to recover, following a diet without fat, spicy food, or coffee, and not even much red meat, and all of that was helping me, but overall, it was a great deal of suffering, that not only a man undergoes, but also women, because there are also many women in the army, and they were also victims of so many offenses and violations.

I was sick with the ulcer for approximately four to six years. I can't remember exactly, but I have the information, the card from my checkups, everything they ended up giving me in the hospital. I keep all of those things because I see it is part of my life story and some day it could be of some help to me. I kept working, employed by the army, even with the problem. And my situation with human rights abuses continued. For them, they see these things as so normal. They work doing it, and they go on with their normal lives, thinking that one doesn't suffer. It doesn't impact them at all anymore. I continued on, being beaten and sick and working, and being beaten and working and working. Six years like that. And my wife knew it. And back then, I only had two children.

On one occasion, we were leaving the military base for an operation we used to do nearby, because it was believed that all the people in the surrounding area were collaborating with the *guerrilla*. So we would go out on lookout, to visit all the small villages outside the military base. I had problems because I couldn't eat the food that we ate, so my wife had the enormous task of bringing me food every day. When I was at the military base I asked permission and it was granted for a short time, but then they forbade my wife bringing me food. But even so, she fought, and tried, and my wife suffered a great deal because of that. I admire her because she is a great woman who fought for me. One day when we left the base for the surrounding areas and she dropped off the food as usual, the official that was in charge of us that day found out. I received the food, I ate, and right when we finished eating and were leaving, they gave me the radio and more weight as a punishment for what I had done. We were heavily equipped and I was carrying my food, and all my clothes. Well, that day, they woke me up in the middle of the night and in addition to the extra weight I had carried they put me on service all night without sleeping.

On another occasion, when they found out I had gone around to the houses nearby to look for food to buy from families because I couldn't eat the food we were carrying, well . . . they assigned a woman to carry out my punishment, on the public road, in plain sight of everyone! They did it with the intention that no one would see them, they would just see the woman, under their orders, punishing me. They took off my shirt, and they had left me in my undershirt with boots, punishing me there, throwing myself down in the mud, and these are situations that I tell you, are very traumatic, that you suffered and will never forget. Many suffered it! I know a lot of friends of mine that were punished. One friend and I were imprisoned sleeping out in the cold at about forty degrees. At night they didn't let us sleep with ponchos, but rather as we were, without a sweater, and sleeping on the floor or sitting up, without covering up, in really small rooms with a really tiny door, locked with a key, and alone there, living through it. I suffered the war within the institution as well. It was hard.

Well, it was easy to get into the military. For them, another member was really good, but to get out, impossible. During the time I was imprisoned, when they would hit me in the stomach, I wanted to inform and report it, as a number of officials advised me to do, to help put an end to it, but that's when I was threatened with death, and told that if I informed the superiors, when I had a time off for furlough, they were going to "disappear" me. The official who beat me called me aside, alone, and told me that, I swear. It was rigid power, really strong. When I was put in the military prison, they did the same with me, saying that if I complained, then when I was in the prison they were going to torture me, and they were going to do it worse, and that they were going to make me "disappear." So, all of this stops you, for fear of losing your life, because of all of the threats.

At that time, due to so much violation, kidnapping, and torture, they created the Human Rights Procurator or Prosecutor, PDH, and shortly after their arrival, the United Nations Verification Mission in Guatemala, MINUGUA, arrived, to finally provide representation from an organization at an international level. That's when the United Nations intervened and arrived and placed a MINUGUA delegation in almost all the Guatemalan departments or states, and they were working in coordination with the Human Rights Procurator. Any violation that was reported to them, any information that they received, was taken down in writing, and then, Human Rights and MINUGUA went to the police, and they went to the army, where they were practically living every day, because that's where they had received the accusations of violations. They arrived at the military bases where they had information that in the military prisons there were soldiers that were suffering and being tortured, but that day the military officials took them out of there, so MINUGUA and Human Rights arrived to see, but there was no one there. As soon as they left, they put them right back in the prison again. So, these are situations that are impossible because they could manipulate the people arriving from MINUGUA. When Human Rights and MINUGUA finally arrived, there started to be, to a certain degree, a little bit of respect, because at that time, with the influence of the United Nations and Congress and the government, there were to be changes in the army laws, and they started to withdraw to a certain degree, and when you wanted to get out, you could leave. I think I probably spent about eight years like that, wanting to leave, but not being able to. I could request it, but they might not have released me, and I couldn't desert because they would have hunted me down, and wherever they found me, they would have killed me on the spot. You are at risk from all sides: from the army, if I deserted, and I was at risk with the *guerrilla,* because I knew, they would see me as a member of the army. Being astute they would capture you, but they wouldn't kill you, so they could start getting information out of you. "This guy is from the army, he's going to tell us what they do, what the situation is in the military base," and they had one! An informant. After they had gotten all the information out of you, they killed you. I had two choices: die or become a member of the *guerrilla.* Some people that had been in the army were captured by the *guerrilla,* and the army saw them informing in the area, and for example they thought the person who had been serving in the military zone had deserted and was now with the *guerrilla,* but it was because the *guerrilla* captured them and took them to get information out of them. They'd say, "Do you want to die, or are you going to become a member of the *guerrilla*?" And so what the army did was make a person disappear, because the truth was that one was a source of information for the *guerrilla.* So, it was a situation with no way out. No way out.

Unemployment, poverty, misery, and so many things obligate one to fall, to a certain degree, into things that one isn't expecting, that one doesn't even imagine are going to happen. After MINU-GUA and Human Rights arrived, the laws started to be a little more flexible, they started releasing the people who wanted to leave the military, and there was no longer any problem leaving, but in a short time, you would be "disappeared." And what was going on? If someone turned up dead, so many miles or so many kilometers out in the mountains, because that's where the dead would be found, what did they say? "The *guerrilla.*" The army would go and take notes for their reports: "At such and such a time, a cadaver was found in such and such a place, with . . ." They were astute, because they would sometimes leave signs such as URNG, Guatemalan National Revolutionary Unit, so that all the people and the press would think that the *guerrilla* had killed them, and not the army. They washed their hands of it, you see? Therefore, one was running a great risk, a very great risk. And it was very difficult, very hard to leave the army and still want to be in Guatemala.

That's why I left my country. I left the army, and for a short time, I was in the city, hidden with my wife. We had three children, but the thing is that one is so uneasy after getting out of the military, and with fear, that I would go out, and I would run into the civil patrols, and the army cars, and there would be flyers from the army thrown about that said that the *guerrilla* had disappeared in Guatemala, but the *guerrilla* continues. Even recently it has been able to secure posts in political parties, and there are even members of the *guerrilla* in Congress. They are still working, doing their job, and they continue. It's the same situation in the country; there is fear of losing one's life at any moment.

So, as a result of this, I asked myself what I should do. I made the decision that I had to leave my family, something very difficult, extremely difficult for me. I think that at the age my children are at, it is the age when they most need me. The oldest is nineteen, the girl is fourteen, almost a woman, and the little one is ten years old. They long to be with me. I left there almost four years ago now. I arrived here as an illegal. The trip is really hard because so many things happen to you along the way. Suffering, hunger, exhaustion, and so many things, but they are things, I think, that each day that goes by, help you to understand life, to understand that in life one has to suffer. Being in the army and having suffered so many things I am trying to forget, things that shouldn't have happened, and just as I might have my life story, many other people have one too, because of their past experiences.

Who would have imagined that this clean-cut man, standing tall with his well-trimmed mustache, a faithful lay assistant in his church, was holding all of this anguish in his heart? Somehow, he has found a place to work toward something he can believe in. Possibly this is the only thing that seems pure and right to him, after all he's been through. Who would have thought this? Do the townspeople here even imagine the anguish these immigrants continue to experience because of past events?

José told me this story in 2005. He finished telling me this disturbing account, in hushed tones, and then we let some silence seep around the edges of our long conversation, creating a body of water for the island of his memories to start drifting away upon. After a long while, I broke the silence to tell him how glad I was that his body had let him know that everything that was happening to him was not right, and that unfortunately, the men inflicting the pain on him had lost sight of what was right and wrong. Slowly shaking his head back and forth, he quietly asked me how one human being can do something so awful to another human being. I felt like I had to answer, I had to attempt to make sense of it all. I said what came to me, that my theory is that some people have a lot of pain and hostility inside, and that in situations like military activities, it all comes to the surface and they need a place to put it. Often times inflicting pain on others and seeing them devastated is a way to mirror back what an imbalanced person feels when they are locked inside themselves. This is the best way I could explain why human beings hurt other human beings: because deep down inside we all share a common pain and hostility, some housing much more than others.

We both fell silent again, looking out over the tender green shoots at the edge of the lawn. The grass had that effervescent glow that it has only in spring, when the tiny new growth has pushed up out of the black soil to start anew. Rebirth. We looked at the place where the shining lime green grass meets the white pavement of the sidewalk. We barely moved, and I stayed with him in silence, contemplating his truth, shouldering the pain that comes with all things beyond comprehension or explanation, sitting on the metal patio furniture on the cement porch of the rectory, with its chipped gray paint exposing the white concrete below, in the middle of this small, rural city, surrounded by grain elevators, silos, railroad tracks, and the smell of the meatpacking plants somewhere in the distance. It was such a quiet place, and I was so glad that he was so far away from the physical place where he nearly lost his health, his life, and all hope to continue living. When I listened to the recording again, transcribing it, I could hear two boys playing ball in the street nearby. When one of them sunk his weathered tennis shoe into the depth of the ball, the explosive thuds on the tape suddenly frightened me, and I jumped, thinking it was the military coming for him, but then I soothingly realized it was just two boys, playing ball, on a street that has little or no traffic, in a small midwestern city, and I sighed, relaxing again and settling back down into the seriousness of José's testimony about serving in the Guatemalan military.

The Aftermath of War

The majority of those killed in the Guatemalan war were the indigenous poor. José states he is Ladino. The women interviewed are Mayan indigenous. Rigoberta Menchú explains this difference between Ladino and indigenous:

> In Guatemala the division between Indians and ladinos has contributed to our situation. And it's certain that in our hearts this has affected us very badly. Ladinos are mestizos, the children of Spaniards and Indians who speak Spanish. But they are in the minority. There is a larger percentage of Indians. Some say it is 60 percent, others that it's 80 percent. We don't know the exact number for a very good reason—there are Indians who don't wear Indian clothes and have forgotten their languages, so they are not considered Indians. And there are middle-class Indians who have abandoned their traditions. They aren't considered Indians either. However this ladino minority thinks its blood is superior, a higher quality, and they think of Indians as a sort of animal. That's the mark of discrimination. The ladinos try to tear off this shell which imprisons them—being the children of Indians and Spaniards. They want to be something different, they don't want to be a mixture. They never mention this mixed blood now.[4]

I have also heard Guatemalans define Ladinos as those who deny their indigenous blood. The hatred with which some Ladinos treat the Mayans cannot be denied, and the racism underlying the genocidal war is still omnipresent in Guatemala. And the Mayan women in Nebraska can feel this hatred that has filtered within, and they actively seek out ways to overcome it, so they can raise children who no longer feel such inferiority.

José's account of the war inside the military allows an opportunity for reflection, in an effort to understand the past, to learn from it, and to acknowledge the reality that has led some to emigrate. All armed conflict has a circular, interrelated nature on this planet. Analyzing the motives behind war, as well as the transnational migrations caused by the poverty that war leaves in its aftermath, gives an opportunity to identify and evaluate international political and economic practices.

The long civil war in Guatemala ended officially in 1996 when the Guatemalan government and the URNG signed the Peace Accords. In 1999 an international truth commission, the *Comisión para el Esclarecimiento Histórico* (CEH), The Historical Clarification Commission, established through the Oslo Accords in 1994, issued its report: *Guatemala, Memoria del Silencio,* Guatemala, Memory of Silence. The commission spent eighteen months painfully reviewing the evidence of genocide, torture, systematic rape, and extermination of Mayan communities during scorched earth operations that destroyed homes, cattle, and crops. The commission examined the role of the United States in the conflict and found that the anticommunist, conservative bent in U.S. policies was backed by those in power in Guatemala, who were rewarded with support for their military regimes, assistance in reinforcing their intelligence, and military training for the counterinsurgents, thus causing the violations of human rights that took place during the armed conflict.[5]

One massacre in Dos Erres, detailed in the report, tells of the unimaginable violence perpetrated by human beings. People were "disappeared," tortured, mutilated, burned alive, or forced to join the military. Children were thrown against walls or into pits and covered with dead adult bodies to kill them. Miscarriages were provoked, fetuses cut from wombs, and women were systematically raped before they were killed.[6]

This massacre included the murder of 252 peasants in 1982 in the community of Dos Erres, La Libertad, Petén, in the north. The military had arrived in the village looking for weapons they accused the *guerrilla* of stealing, and then proceeded to massacre at least 250 people, causing the hundreds of survivors to flee in exile. Based on investigations, testimony, and DNA samples, the court summoned eighteen former soldiers in 2000, although the legal suit began in 1994. FAMDEGUA, Association of Relatives of the Detained-Disappeared of Guatemala, says that seven of the eighteen military personnel responsible for the genocide have been captured.[7] The Dos Erres trial resulted in sentencing Pedro Pimentel to 6,060 years of prison, 30 years for each of the 201 assassinations and 30 additional years for crimes against humanity. In 2011, for the first time in Guatemalan history, four retired military were summoned as well, to answer for this massacre.

In 2012, former military dictator Efraín Ríos Montt—accused of commanding that Indian villages be razed decades ago during the civil war—was ordered by a Guatemalan judge to stand trial on charges of genocide and crimes against humanity. The military's actions against indigenous communities were the focus of allegations, as the prosecution outlined seventy-two separate episodes that resulted in the deaths of at least 1,771 people. In an effort to heal the past, the Guatemalan Forensic Anthropological Foundation has exhumed the remains of nearly 6,000 bodies of massacre victims, and their relatives await legal procedures to bring army officials to court to face charges. In 2013 Ríos Montt was found guilty of genocide during his 1982 to 1983 dictatorship and was sentenced to eighty years in prison. Some now question whether former president Otto Pérez Molina, a retired military officer, may also be implicated.

The CEH report relays a deep concern over the evidence of torture and names two fundamental consequences of its systematic use on a community. First, training and teaching people to be experts in the most efficient and ghastly forms of torture, intended to break the victims down both physically and spiritually, has lasting and devastating effects on society. Second, incorporating torture within the routine of the state's military and police forces, and especially intelligence operations, makes torture so "normal" that it is tolerated by society and judicial officials.[8] José mentioned this normalcy in his testimony. To me, inflicting pain on another person results in eventual consequences, and incorrect behavior definitely accrues psychological debts for both parties involved. These outcomes provoke the silences, the spaces where the Mayan immigrants have learned not to go, and they bid me not to ask. However, their silence says as much as words. The stuttering and stammering from the oral interviews do not appear in this written testimonial. One woman stutters constantly, and has a difficult time catching her breath, and I am sure this is some form of post-traumatic stress and panic, either directly from war, or from the resulting experience of intense poverty that led to their emigration. Others trail off into inaudible mumbling when they get to parts of the stories where they fade out and can't talk. There is much here that is unspeakable, that can't be revisited, that is simply untouchable. Their protective mechanism of silence has been passed down over generations, starting perhaps at the time of the conquest. The Mayan legacy is an oral history that cannot be stolen or usurped, orality being one cultural form of self-preservation. Hopefully, in telling their stories the Mayans interviewed arrive at a better understanding of themselves.

Martha and the Postwar Reorganization Committees

Martha used her strength and knowledge to help reconstruct Guatemalan society in the aftermath of war. She understands the underlying social stigmas and hardships the Mayan indigenous women have faced, having worked on numerous postwar commissions. Unlike most of her Mayan female counterparts in Nebraska, Martha was educated and professionally employed in Guatemala. Here she outlines her postwar leadership role as an indigenous Mayan woman:

When the Peace Accords were signed, COPMAGUA, Coordinator of the Mayan People's Organizations of Guatemala, needed a facilitator for the National Indigenous Women's Commission. I applied and was hired, so I stepped down from my teaching position. While I was a facilitator for the National Indigenous Women's Commission I began inviting women from all of the different organizations, among them the women of Kaqla, and the women's group Konojel, who, unfortunately, sometimes participated, but later withdrew. The Academy of Mayan Languages of Guatemala, ALMG, was invited, but never participated. Those that participated in the group were the organizations that were members of the IUCM, Instance of Unity and Consensus Maya, and Tukum Umam Council, and UPMAG, the Mayan People's Union, all of whom have a presence in the villages, municipalities, and provinces.

I then became a member of the Technical Negotiation Unit where my principal responsibility was to facilitate the necessary tools to advance the orders of the eight permanent national commissions of COPMAGUA, which were created to ensure completion of the Indigenous People's Identity and Rights Agreement. There were Mayan professionals and university graduates from other countries who had experience and knowledge of the different themes dealing with the indigenous. Many of them participated and supported COPMAGUA, and many of us believed and placed our hopes in them to create the space in which the changes that would transform Guatemala into a multicultural, multilingual, multiethnic country were going to take place.

The communities and organizations of the different provinces supported and endorsed COPMAGUA, and everyone entered in with good intention for the Mayan movement. But, unfortunately, three of the five Mayan orders that made up COPMAGUA had URNG tendencies; one, with Guerrilla Army of the Poor, EGP tendencies, and another, with the Revolutionary Organization of the Armed People, ORPA, and there was another that represented the Rebel Armed Forces, FAR. These three groups seemed to be more politically belligerent than ALMG, whose focus was limited to Mayan languages and didn't allow them to visualize their implication in the other themes related to the indigenous. It seemed to be that the Counsel of Mayan Organizations of Guatemala, the COMG, was focused on participating on the Permanent National Commission of Education and temporarily participated on the Commission for Women. The other three instances took advantage of this type of participation to imbalance Mayan political power, moving towards a political empowerment for URNG, and in the end it was common to see a flag of the URNG party inside the COPMAGUA installations even though it was prohibited to place a flag from any other political party there. This frustrated the hopes that the Mayan movement had placed in COPMAGUA, and many Mayan leaders ended up stepping down because the space created and backed by the diverse Mayan organizations no longer represented the ideals of the Mayan movement. It became a political platform for URNG rather than a political platform for the Mayan movement.

Those experiences have helped me a lot. In COPMAGUA there was no work schedule. Sometimes we met until ten o'clock at night, or we would work until the sun came up, but without caring about the time. We did it convinced that the work was to benefit women and that it was something we liked to do. I started with COPMAGUA with such a desire to support, to contribute something, and I know that many people arrived the same way. We believed in a space that was ours, in working to benefit our people, working with honor, responsibility and transparency, the way it is done in our communities, and not for money, nor for personal interests. But along the way, I realized there was pressure from a different angle. There was distrust, tension, because many felt a lot of resentment that none of us had anything to do with, but for them, any person who did not share their political ideology, was therefore against them, they were an enemy and they pressured, and pressured, until they were able to get you to leave the job.

I stepped down. I continued studying in the university, towards a master's degree in political science, in an effort to understand how the state structure works. People want immediate change, but they don't know that there are processes that have to be followed. A person has to go through many channels before the proposal arrives to Congress and is discussed, analyzed, added to or changed, and is approved by all the representatives before it can become a law.

After that I worked in a peace program of the Organization of American States, the OEA/Propaz. What the program intended was to have indigenous representation, of men, of different cultures, and from the right. That's where they began. But then another topic came up, and that's when I realized that it was more than a tendency. They wanted to make it something national. They told me my contract was up, but the indigenous organizations had already told me they were going to take me out, that I wasn't one of them. They are not from the Left. They wanted representation from business owners more than people from the Left. Maybe it was discrimination. I am unsure.

Martha continued her work, assisting with other peace processes, but repeatedly, she would see that there was bullying and self-interest, and she would step aside, knowing many of the people were still armed back in their communities and were pushing their own agenda forward with mere words, for now, rather than seeking out the middle ground in the peace processes. Rather than point out their discrimination and silencing of other viewpoints, somewhat out of physical fear as well as simply being realistic about how far the process would actually be able to organically unfold, she decided to seek other opportunities in the United States.

Martha visited our Spanish class at MCC in Omaha to talk about her work as an indigenous woman on the Peace Commissions and detail some of the atrocities from the CEH report. She broke down after telling us the military cut off a woman's breasts and played ball with them in a public plaza, and we silently shouldered part of the sorrow with her. Acknowledging the past events somehow begins the healing process of historical memory.

In a 1999 visit, former president William Clinton officially apologized to the Guatemalan people for the U.S. role in the conflict and the atrocities committed as outlined in the CEH report. American officials had previously endorsed the findings of the panel, but no president had directly confronted the issue as Clinton did, stating, "The United States will no longer take part in campaigns of repression."[9] I recall seeing him on television shortly after this visit, twisting a woven bracelet that Mayan women had given to him around his wrist, and stating its significance to him. Forgiveness begins with admission of past misdeeds, and enhances a plea for absolution to those who have been mistreated.

Violence is still present in Guatemala. As of mid-2011, the Human Rights Procurator stated that thirty-two people in the electoral campaign had been assassinated, and a news article reported a violence level that remains high, with Guatemala having an average of eighteen homicides a day by powerful drug cartels and youth gangs.[10] The country boasts the highest number of security officials employed, a profession that has become highly utilized worldwide, yet 90 percent of all crimes are not solved. The socioeconomic divide between rich and poor is a major cause of the violence. And with all that has happened in Guatemala, to ensure the success of the peace process, is the country now at peace? José laments the continued violence, the underlying reason why so many Mayan Guatemalan indigenous men and women have searched elsewhere for economic stability and a peaceful existence:

> Women in Guatemala continue to live this whole same situation. There are still deaths, tortures, and there is a large percentage, in some sectors of Guatemala, of women being raped, kidnapped, tortured, killed . . . it is very difficult, but maybe those of us Guatemalans that are here in the U.S., we have a different story of our lives.
>
> On a daily basis indigenous women try to have a post in the government or in some institutions because necessity itself is

making women awaken and search out their place in Guatemala. Women, each day more and more, feel a great necessity to attain support regarding their race, their culture, and their way of living too, because women are still being marginalized, even in their own homes.

In Guatemala, if a woman works as a police officer at the national level, she is under the control of her bosses, and they do whatever they want with her. If a pretty woman arrives, first she has to be the big boss's girlfriend, or pretend to have a relationship with him. There are so many agonies. And in many cases, out of necessity itself, women have to put up with so many things that are perhaps hidden. Women suffered, put up with, and continue to put up with so much because every day in Guatemala, misery, poverty, every kind of situation, obligates women to sometimes be under the control of a certain system, under a certain power, and it is out of necessity itself. And possibly, it is because of this situation itself that women were living that they are emigrating from one place to another.

Another really difficult thing that happens in Guatemala, perhaps also because of unemployment, is that the homes break apart because there aren't any jobs, there's nothing to eat in the families, a lot of clashes start happening, there are many conflicts within the family, the wife ends up leaving the husband, and ending up with the children, the woman has to emigrate, she has to fight for her children, and has to keep moving forward. There are so many things that one lives. We keep suffering each day with such great clamor.

The violence caused by armed conflict alters and continues to disintegrate society. In listening to the Guatemalan immigrant stories we note the need humans have to be heard by others, to be heeded.

Although globalization and international trade agreements allow some goods to move more freely, the Mayans and other immigrants do not enjoy the luxury of being able to travel freely between countries and economic systems because human beings simply do not share the same privilege as commodities. Possibly the Mayans are willing to share their stories because they know that in listening to one another we create more understanding and more tolerance of one another and the realities and needs we each bring to the table.

Physical, economical, and emotional warfare leaves a population impoverished and replete with violence. Unfair politics and imbalanced world economies are what Noam Chomsky labeled "class warfare."[11] It truly is a war on humanity. Recall the United Nations Charter, signed in 1945. The Statute of the International Court of Justice is an integral part of the Charter, focused on saving succeeding generations from the scourge of war through reaffirming fundamental human rights and the worth of all human persons, practicing tolerance and living together in peace without using armed force, and promoting the economic and social advancement of all peoples.[12]

Possibly we need to heed the call of the United Nations. We must take a look at history and stop the repetition of arms production, sales, distribution, and use. José was a soldier in a genocidal war caused by defined economic interests and gains for the United States. Is it a war that needed to occur? And what were the circular results of that war in terms of U.S. economic production and the labor pool that enhances it? Although they were both educated and gainfully employed, both José and Martha, out of impotence, fear, and hope, opted to leave Guatemala and seek out a better life in the United States. The next chapter describes how the other women arrived at a similar decision. It recounts the difficulty of the journey itself, and what happened once they arrived on U.S. soil to start a new life.

3

The Journey to El Norte

I drag my wheeled suitcases through the muddy slush on the side-walks, pull out of the Omaha airport, and start heading onto the back roads, a little apprehensive because it is a dark, damp, autumn night. The black leafless branches of trees are all dripping, a light fog lingers in the air, and fallen leaves dot brown grass edged with nearly melted snow. I'm afraid to be alone on these roads, but as soon as I get on the flat piece of highway leading to Fremont and Columbus I suddenly feel as if I'm floating above the plains. A sense of intense expansiveness enters into me as I glide along this tiny strip of two-lane highway through the scantily populated Nebraska flatlands. The "great plains" allow you to see for miles in every direction, and household or farm lights glisten here and there, giving a sense of accompaniment. The highway unfurls a farmhouse now and then, surrounded by low-slung, round, cone-roofed silos, perched next to garage-like structures housing equip-ment. Often there's a red barn. Irrigation contraptions run the length of the fields and in the dark of night appear to be some kind of prehistoric monstrosity moving too closely toward the highway. Then fields, and more fields, and lights sparkling in the distance, illuminating more signs of life. Once in a while a giant grain elevator accompanied by groups of looming silos heaves up out of the plains like something suddenly appearing in a science fiction film. The highway, homes, and grain elevators all hug the railroad tightly, answering the subsistent need to move oneself and the bounty taken from one's land along to others.

Although it is night, the meatpacking plants are well lit and smoke emits from the tops of the buildings and smokestacks, manifesting they are still in full function. Trucks continue pulling in and out from these luminous conglomerations and sliding slowly onto untraversed back highways, heading toward larger highways, now empty of their cargo of cattle on the way to slaughter. This is big business. It never stops. The three shifts the Mayans alternately work prove this.

There is a calm quiet on these back roads and in these small cities. In the morning, as I drive through the farmland to get to the towns, coal-black cows dot the dry fields with stubs of cornstalks. The cows glean what they can from the chopped-off stalks, and I pause to soak in the hay color against the black cows. The smell of manure lingers in the air as country roads weave through one and another feedlot interspersed among drying cornfields and plots dotted with harvested bales of hay. Trains slice through the center of the towns and cities, speeding along in both directions all day long. The flatness of Nebraska allows you to admire all the multicolored cars at once, lining their way across the now golden plains, moving the bounty.

Life is just simpler and not so urgent as in big cities. People have more time. The friendliness in the airport—the Nebraskan hospitality that easily hands over time to make small talk—and the accompanying desire to please others are experienced from the moment the plane touches ground, and extend from the airport to the grocers, to the taco truck, and at last, to the monastery.

On this crisp autumn morning Martha and I sat down at her kitchen table covered with a floral print plastic tablecloth that allows for quick cleanups after she feeds her children. The garden plot outside was drying up, and the brown leaves that had fallen from the trees were flying about on a wild rampage throughout the neighborhood. While we were talking, a door off the kitchen slowly drifted open and another Guatemalan Mayan woman appeared in the kitchen. She didn't make eye contact and soundlessly headed toward the sink where she began tidying up. Martha didn't acknowledge her presence, so neither did

I. A bit later a young man appeared at the back door, and rather than knocking, stood looking in at us through the window. The other woman glided over, opened the door, and took a plastic, ball-shaped bag from him. Their communication was wordless, and he vanished once again.

This woman put a wrought iron *comal*, a flat iron griddle, on the gas stove and turned it on. She then slowly, and very quietly, opened the plastic bag, separated a bit of *masa*, corn dough, and started softly patting at it in the palms of her hands, turning it to and fro, in a constant spiral movement, molding it into a small, circular, thick Guatemalan tortilla. She worked silently, preparing the tortillas, heating them on the *comal*, and then setting them one on top of the other in a small, round, towel-lined basket. Once finished, she faded through the door to our right again, without exchanging any words or eye contact.

The Decision to Emigrate

At the end of our interview Martha opened the same door that the silent woman had disappeared through, and in a few minutes she reappeared. Martha said, "Anna, this is María. She would like to tell you how she ended up here as well," and so she did:

I'm from Guatemala, from the same place as Martha, except she lived in town and I lived in a village. We didn't know each other there. I arrived and stayed with some relatives, but then I moved around until I came here to live, and that's when I met her.

In Guatemala I studied so that I would be able to earn enough money to eat. I worked in a chewing gum factory in Guatemala, first packing the gum, and then I was supervisor of the trucks with containers going to different countries. With just one year of studies left, the boss promoted me to secretary, and then he gave me an exportation post. I received the calls from different countries and took their wholesale orders. I earned a little more money then, and half was for me, and half for my dad, but I talked to my boss about my salary and my expenses, telling him I didn't have enough for food, clothes, housing, and for my parents, so he raised my salary, but it still wasn't enough.

I don't have brothers or sisters or my mom or dad here. My family is in Guatemala. I arrived here all by myself. Since my dad's a peasant, he doesn't have much money so unless an American shows up and helps us out by giving us money, we are poor. So, I said, "I'm going to El Norte, to the United States." In the beginning he didn't want to let me go, because I'm a woman, and something could happen to me on the way, as happens with the Mexicans. Crossing the border is so difficult! He told me I couldn't go, but then later I was able to convince him. I told him, "It's that we don't have money. Maybe I should go there," and he finally gave me his permission. The truth is, if I arrived here, it's out of necessity, because I want to help my dad. I have five more brothers and sisters. One sister is already married, and the other sister is older and has a daughter, but the others are younger than me. I have one brother that's eight years old, the other is twelve, and I need to support them, so that they can complete their studies, so that one day they will have a job. I want to help them.

Again, poverty was the driving force in her decision to head to El Norte. Even leaving her village to find work in the capital was not lucrative enough to help her family get out of poverty. María could not leave her country until she had her father's blessing or permission, a common Mayan and Latino tradition. Most families do not want their children to go to El Norte; they know some die on the journey, that life will be difficult, and their children and family unit will never be the same again without all their offspring together. But in the end, they succumb, finally worn down by the pressing reality of their material need, thus releasing their young in the hopes of survival.

Many undocumented workers in the United States have experienced this period of wavering back and forth about their decision. Manuela describes the same thoughts that led her to leave:

1. A billboard outside the JBS plant in Grand Island, Nebraska, that shows JBS employees dressed for the cutting floor, wearing clear safety glasses and safety helmets.

2. Trucks arriving at the JBS plant in Grand Island.

3. Oromex Jeweler and the historic Grand Theatre in downtown Grand Island

4. The Downtown Center in the Grand Island city center

5. Boutiques, shopping, and the historic courthouse in downtown Grand Island

6. Bales of hay and an irrigation system in Columbus, Nebraska.

7. Cattle being raised for slaughter in Columbus.

8. Cattle glean the last corn out of dry fields as ADM-Columbus Corn Processing, an ethanol plant that processes corn into a variety of feed and food products in Columbus, towers in the distance.

9. Trucks line up to deliver corn to ADM in Columbus.

10. The Cargill plant in Columbus.

11. The signage outside the Cargill plant in Columbus states "¡Ahora estamos contratando!," [We are hiring now!] and urges readers to "Pick up your application here!"

12. A mural in downtown Columbus that highlights days on the prairie and the importance of trains for transporting grain and other commodities.

13. A plaza in the center of downtown Columbus.

14. A main street in downtown Columbus.

15. Leaving Columbus on Highway 30.

16. The sheriff's truck, water tower, and grain elevator in the heart of Schuyler, Nebraska.

17. Restaurant, pupusería (place serving Salvadoran corn cakes filled with beans, cheese or meat), and tortillería (tortilla shop) "La Gloria" in downtown Schuyler. The "Chichihualco Super Market" is named after a city in the south of Mexico and carries Mexican and Guatemalan products. "El Paisano," the Countryman store with check-cashing services and electronics, is flanked by a pioneer days mural in downtown Schuyler.

18. U.S. post office and police department in downtown Schuyler.

19. Cargill plant outside of Schuyler.

20. Trailer park right next to the Cargill plant in Schuyler.

21. Silo next to cattle gleaning dry fields outside of Schuyler.

22. Mountains of corn outside Fremont, Nebraska.

23. The Great Plains as seen near Fremont.

24. Silos next to the railroad tracks near Fremont.

25. Fremont Beef Company in Fremont.

26. Hormel Foods in Fremont.

27. (*Opposite top*) Multicolored sashes worn as belts by Mayan women.

28. (*Opposite bottom*) The Mayan women's *huipil*, or woven blouse, displaying the sun outlined with the Mayan calendar day symbols.

29. (*Above*) Sun design on a Mayan woman's *huipil* from Chichicastenango, Guatemala.

30. Mayan children display regional Mayan dress and a *marimba*, the national instrument of Guatemala.

31. Mayan children in Nebraska don regional Mayan dress for a special celebration.

I was born in a small town, in a village. There are a lot of people that come here, so my sister told me to come. She came to be with her husband here, and I came to be with her. My Dad was sick, and I wondered where I was going to get 20,000 *quetzales* [$2,525]. It's a lot of money. My dad said we could use the deed from our plot of land, or from our house, or apply for a loan from the bank. My sister's father-in-law went to take out a loan, and that's how I was able to come here five years ago. After I started working, I went to each room where they called me, and I started paying back the money. Now I don't owe anything anymore.

The type of work Manuela did to repay such a large sum of money was not apparent.

Juana shared this common curiosity to find out if life would actually be easier in El Norte, as everyone was reporting back in Guatemala:

I have been in the U.S. for five years, and for three here in Nebraska. I came here because I wanted to see it for myself, because there are a lot of people who say there's a lot of money here in the United States. The people that come here return to Guatemala, and they build a house or they buy a car, and you can see that they have money. I came here, and I think it's true, there is a lot of money here, but only when you have your papers. Otherwise you can't work and you don't have health insurance. It depends on each state, because there are companies that don't ask for your papers.

From firsthand experience Juana has learned that there is more earning power in the United States, but it is inaccessible to the undocumented who cannot enter the workforce legally. Through their kinship networks they begin researching work possibilities for the undocumented, as well as how to buy papers and start accessing U.S. dollars.

Each woman describes her journey toward wealth. Martha's focus was different in assessing her decision to leave Guatemala. She arrived by plane on a fiancée visa, while the others had to make the trip wholly on foot or by bus, with the last leg by car or air. She details:

> My husband is from Guatemala, from a neighboring village. When I was studying in elementary school I met him, but then he left to come here and I stayed there studying. We weren't married or in love. When we were fifteen years old we were friends, and then, he would always come seek me out every time he came to Guatemala. We have known each other for ten or twelve years. I took my time deciding what I was going to do with my life. I knew that this isn't like a profession, that if you don't like it, you can just change it and nothing will happen. I had different options, but I chose him because of his way of thinking, his values, and principles. Personally, I believe that as fundamental pillars a family should have values and principles, and love of God. Without them, there is a void in the person and many want to fill it with addiction, or by womanizing and having children outside of marriage, and that isn't the right path. He had his primary education, and he finished his secondary here, and got his GED, and now he is studying management at the community college. I know there is a way for me to study here as well. I have the admissions application for the university, but because of the children, I can't. My husband is a citizen here. He has been here for years. So in the end, I got a visa to come here. They gave me residency for two years, and then they will allow me another two years.

The Border Crossing

The other women arrived differently. María details the need for stamina, a false identity, and considerable cash throughout the journey:

> Now I send my family money every month, because they need money, but I got deep into debt with my dad when I left, and I owe him about $9,000. It's so much money because I got caught in Mexico, and the immigration officials fined me 3,000 pesos [$1,000].

You give them the money so they will let you go through. Luckily, I brought a lot of money from Guatemala, and they know that, and that you want to cross over, so they ask you for more money. The day Mexican police officers sent me back I was in Chihuahua, but I didn't tell them I was from Guatemala. When they asked where I was from I said Chiapas. I had papers from Mexico too, but when they asked where I wanted to go and I said I was sightseeing, they sent me back to Chiapas. But I didn't go. They take you to the terminal and they show you the bus that goes to Chiapas. They pay for the bus, and leave you on it. I went with them, but I knew I wasn't going to go to Chiapas. I just started heading towards Chihuahua again. We all did it.

They made about 15,000 pesos in fines [$5,000]. For Mexicans that is a lot of money. It's all because of the border. The Salvadorans, the Nicaraguans . . . we all have to go through Mexico to get to the U.S., and we already know that's why the Mexicans have more money than our countries do, because they steal so much money from migrants.

Traveling from Guatemala to the U.S. border was a thirteen-day journey. And other than the desert, I walked two nights, I think. We then came by car. Another man, a *coyote*, a border smuggler, brought me from Guatemala, and he told us which way to go, and another *coyote* guided us to the U.S. The *coyote* from Guatemala left us at the Mexico border, and the *coyote* from California took us from the Mexican border into the U.S., and that *coyote* made us walk in the desert because we couldn't go by car anymore. We traveled thirteen days, sometimes in a van, and sometimes by bus. I traveled on my own, alone, but there were about fifteen people in the group. I barely got to know them; we were from different places, and we were going to different places. One was going to Georgia, another to California, and another to Miami. One person asked me where I was going and I told them San Diego, and they were going to Miami, and that's how it goes. Another person asked me where I was from so I told them Soloma, and they were from San Juan, a tiny village, and someone else was from

Santa Eulalia. That's how it went. We are from different places, but we don't get to know each other more than that.

On those trips it's mixed, there are men and women going together, and some of them come with their husbands or wives too. You travel wondering how it's going, or asking yourself what the desert will be like or if it will be difficult to arrive. Now, I realize, if Immigration caught me here, and deported me to Guatemala, I would never come back again, because I already suffered so much in the desert! The desert might be the most terrible thing that exists on earth! You fall down on gravel, on rocks, your knees are skinned, your feet get hurt, everything is covered in dirt, you .... [Her voice is shaking, on the brink of tears.] I suffered A LOT, a lot from that, and right now I tell my dad, "Never, ever again." If Immigration caught and deported me, I would never come here ever again, because I don't ever want to suffer that way, because crossing the border is the worst, it's the most terrible thing that exists in life, and besides that, you have to pay for your food, and if you feel hungry, you have to eat cold food, with only water. You get so tired in the desert, and sometimes the border patrol is hovering in a helicopter above, watching you, and you have to hide under the trees or find a hole. You have to look for some place, or sometimes you hear the border patrol's cars among the hills, and you have to hide so they won't see you, but they stay there for a long time, just standing, and there, right there, you have to wait. I told all of this to my dad and he said to me, "My daughter, how could you take all that?" Now it would hurt me a lot. "Never again," I tell him. "I am in a very beautiful place. The trees look so gorgeous, but to get here, it has been very, very difficult."

In Guatemala, the people tell about how difficult it is to cross the desert, but they come just the same. I knew it was difficult because our neighbors come and go from Ohio. They leave their wives there for two, three years, and then they return to see them. And they always said, "No, the U.S. is difficult. It's beautiful, but crossing over is the worst thing there is. We have money, we have a house, but it has all been so hard for us." And it's true. They tell what the place is like, how they cross the border, how to get here, and how to look for a job if you don't have papers and you don't speak English.

In addition to all the suffering, the people who helped me cross the border charged me $3,000. $3,000! Yes, it's a lot of money, and besides that, they also played a trick on me. They dropped me off, but in Mexico, and some Mexican men called my relatives in San Diego and told them that I had arrived in Phoenix, when I was still on the Mexican side of the border, and my cousin's husband sent them the money. Two days later I called my cousin from Mexico and we realized they had stolen that money. $2,000! So I had to pay the money back to her. And that really hurt me, because I owe money, I don't have money, I don't pay her rent or for food, and that's how my life was when I arrived here. I regretted it all so much. I felt so bad for my dad.

But God is always there to help me move forward. That's what I always said to myself when I was feeling that way. In the end I owed $9,000. And that's what I'm working on now. $9,000! Now I only owe about $2,000. I've been paying it off for two years.

I miss seeing my parents, and that makes it really hard. I only talk to them on the phone. I don't have a mother or children here. I told my mom that I was suffering a lot here, and she gets so sad. Lately, I have realized, really, when you don't have your dad or brothers and sisters here, or relatives that want to support you, it makes you miss them a lot.

Along the way they encounter many detours, setbacks, or "barriers" as María says. Once they arrive in the United States they move about, relocating until they find the place where they can work and start sending money home, to cover the debts accrued to make the journey and also to support their impoverished families. In this odyssey toward survival, many use the unknown terrain of conflicting realities to maneuver, play tricks, and make their own private way toward economic stability. The U.S. border that supposedly prevents undocumented entry is a fictitious wall. The Mexican police and citizens who take advantage of those risking their lives by charging them exorbitant fees or fines, and the gang members and thugs who wait to beat and rob them of their possessions and the crossover money, are all capitalizing on this deception.

It is not surprising the border crossers also have to take their gains and leads, using just as much deception to get where they need to go as those around them are employing. It's the nature of the game of getting ahead, the competition for economic stability, and the rules are very pliable. The journey is so devastating that making it twice becomes an impossibility. Manuela tells:

> I haven't been back to Guatemala yet. I can't because if I leave, I can't come back because crossing over is so hard. I came here walking. We were walking for a long time, and we arrived, but I don't know, I don't remember exactly where, if it was California or Texas. I do remember the moment I arrived in the United States. We were driving in a car, the *coyote*, the men who bring people and return and bring more, took us along the ravines, saying: "This way. We are almost there." My sister crossed that way too. Almost everyone that comes here from Guatemala crosses that way. They go through the desert.
>
> Crossing is really hard, but there are a lot who do it. Little by little, everyone crosses. They all suffer a lot. They give you food and water, but it's not the same as eating at home.

The Mayan women seldom complain or lament their present or past situations; however, in talking about the border-crossing experience they all commented that it is excruciatingly difficult. Juana had it a little easier, arriving before border control was so pervasive:

> I crossed the border to come here. I came on foot, like the wetbacks. When I came, it was quiet and they didn't catch me. Thank God there wasn't as much border patrol then. It's a really long journey. It took me about eight days to get to the border, but eight days

traveling night and day. It is really tiring. You want to sleep, but you only sleep a little bit on the bus until you get to the border. I crossed the border, and then came to Nebraska by plane. When I left my house to come here, I prayed to God, that he would help me arrive to be with my husband. Well, thank God, all is well.

Some mentioned that the *coyotes* give them "vitamins" to boost their energy during the most strenuous parts of the trip, and when one woman suffers numerous miscarriages after her arrival, she worries about the pills' long-term effects. However, once they have handed themselves over to the *coyotes*, they simply follow their instructions and demands.

Lucía tells about her border-crossing experience, again reiterating it is a once-in-a-lifetime experience:

> I asked my cousin to bring me, telling her, "I have my two children. How am I going to get ahead?" She said, "The day you arrive, you arrive with me." I arrived here just like this, on foot. Thank God that we have already gotten through those times. It was about four hours walking in the desert. We left at 1:00 in the morning, and we arrived at 5:30 in the morning. We came out on a highway, and another man arrived to pick us up in a minivan. He got us in. Immigration was going to catch us, but thank God they didn't. We entered so quickly, one after the other, one after the other, and thank God, we arrived in fifteen days, from my village to the United States. It was many days, and after I came, my brother-in-law came. It took him longer, about a month or six weeks. He says they walked about three or four days in the desert and they couldn't cross over because there were so many migrants. We were so very worried about them. However, my cousin came with my husband and he arrived in a month. My husband is from my village; he was my husband there. My cousin arrived, and he told me my brother-in-law would put the money up for me because I didn't have the money. And some friends, a couple, came with me. I left my son there with my mom. He was one year old when I left him. *Ay,* my mom . . . she was holding

him in her arms always, because there, in Guatemala, we carry the child in a multicolored woven square like this [wrapped up and tied on the front or back], she carried him like this, until my son started walking. My mother was doing the most possible for my son. I always thank her because she helped so much with raising my children. She suffered a lot because I came over here. And now things are going really well for me, thank God.

Guatemalan immigrants pay *coyotes* anywhere from $2,000 to $12,000 to arrive at and cross the U.S. border. Transnational migrations affect all countries involved. Migrants report they carry very little because they expect to be attacked and robbed throughout their journey: "Many face kidnap, rape and murder at the hands of criminal gangs, often in collusion with authorities, during their passage through Mexico."[1] Often the *coyotes* that receive pay for transporting migrants across the borders also commit crimes against them along the way, knowing that migrants cannot report their offenses, or that officials will overlook injustices because they are paid off or fear retaliation from organized criminal rings. "Those responsible for the abuses are rarely held to account and many cases of abducted or murdered migrants are not adequately investigated."[2]

Calculating the numbers of those crossing Central America is impossible, but Amnesty International states that 60,000 people were detained in Mexico in 2011, and nine of ten migrants were from Central America. They continue:

In February 2011, the National Human Rights Commission reported that 11,000 migrants had been kidnapped in the previous six months. Throughout 2011, migrant rights defenders have been subject to attack, death threats and intimidation in reprisal for their efforts to support migrants. Fray Tomas, who runs "La 72" migrants' shelter in Tenosique, Tabasco state, has received anonymous death threats over the phone and been insulted by state police and members of the military. During Mexico's appearance before the U.N. Committee on the Protection of all Migrant

Workers in April 2011, it was clear that the government lacked a concrete plan of action to tackle the migrants' rights crisis in the country.[3]

As of 2010 there were nearly twelve million Mexican and 800,000 Guatemalan immigrants living in the United States, and 34 percent of the Mexican and 48 percent of the Guatemalan immigrants arrived in 2000 or later.[4] According to the IOM, 11 percent of the Guatemalan population live in the United States, and 30 percent are women.[5] "Statistics from the General Directorate of Migration show that in 2011, 30,855 Guatemalans were forcibly returned by air from the United States and 31,427 by land from Mexico. Upon their return to the country, migrants face myriad difficulties and obstacles to their successful reintegration, such as limited economic opportunities and the lack of access to formal education, social services and credit. The persistence of these conditions which pushed them away from Guatemala in the first place compounded with the 'failed' voyage produces low self-esteem and emotional problems in many returnees."[6]

Central American countries claim they are trying to remedy the problems and hardships caused by circular transnational migrations. Land access is also a major component of indigenous peoples' poverty and therefore migration. A Minority Rights Group International report states Guatemalans need land redistribution, access, and protection, as well as improved wages and working conditions, to stay in their country of origin and make a living. As it is, in Guatemala "less than 1 per cent of export-oriented agricultural producers still control 75 per cent of the best land, leaving indigenous people to continue to seek wage labour through internal and external seasonal migration."[7]

The Mayan women's lives have been directly affected by global economic policy, war, and staggeringly poor postwar local economies. Emigration commenced in the 1950s and established familial and friendship networks that have welcomed subsequent waves of immigrants throughout the late 1970s and early 1980s, opening a highway to economic security. Community is at the core as immigrants facilitate movement and access to economic gain for one another. The border crossing, in my opinion, is an experience caused by poverty that was worsened after armed conflicts in Central America, and the border has become so dangerous that it is analogous to war.[8]

Documentation

U.S. citizens do not need a visa for a stay of ninety days or less in Guatemala, and they can apply to Guatemalan immigration to extend their stay an additional ninety days. In 2006, Guatemala, El Salvador, Honduras, and Nicaragua entered the "Central America-4 (CA-4) Border Control Agreement," allowing nationals to travel freely across land borders between the countries without any entry or exit requirements at immigration checkpoints. U.S. citizens may also move freely between the four countries with a valid visa.

Policies are not this open for Guatemalans intent on entering the United States, although thirty-seven countries participate in the Visa Waiver Program, VWP, which grants a visitor [B] visa holder stays of ninety days or less without obtaining a visa if the travelers meet eligibility requirements.[9] None of the Central or South American countries are eligible to participate in the VWP.

Most of the Mayans seek out a petition from a relative to legalize their situation. The U.S. Department of State's Bureau of Consular Affairs tries to process naturalization cases within five months and mediate relative petitions for a spouse, parent, or minor child of a U.S. citizen within six months. However, often the volume of petitions makes these goals impossible to meet. If the women had applied for a tourist visa from the American embassy in Guatemala it would have been a lengthy and costly process, and because of their poverty, most likely their applications would have been denied. There are many types of visas, and application fees vary.[10] However, the Mayans do not want a tourist visa; they need a green card, which offers permanent residency to live and work in the United States for as long as desired. Some-times officials from the Guatemalan consulate visit meatpacking plants or the local union offices to offer consulate services, Gua-temalan passports, or documentation, knowing it is much eas-ier for the Mayan workers than traveling to Denver, Colorado, to solicit their services. The local Catholic priest petitioned for his acolyte José and managed to get him a work permit and res-ident visa, documents that would allow him to return home for his mother's death and then come back and petition for his wife and children, but this appeared to be a quite special case. José tells about his paperwork dilemma:

> I came to Nebraska because I had acquaintances here. But at the beginning of this year my mother was dying so I told the priest. We went to Immigration and I asked for a permit to leave the coun-try for the death of my mother. I think it must have been a really special situation. Father was with me, doing a lot for me, going all over the place, and I left the country, went to my mother's burial, and returned legally. I'm not undocumented anymore. They legal-ized my status. But I can't process the papers and petition to bring my wife and children until I qualify and am granted residency.
>
> I actually went to Guatemala with *dos corazones*, with two hearts. I went to say goodbye to my mother. When I got there she was unconscious, but still alive. I arrived two days before she died. It was really sad to see my mother in that situation, and at her burial, but I was happy perhaps because on the other hand I got to go and see my wife and my children. It's really hard, for my wife, who told me not to come back here, or better yet, to take them with me! They all wanted to come with me. I was in Guatemala for almost two months. I asked permission for three weeks but Immigration gave me two months, so I took advan-tage so I could be there with my family, and I brought my dad back with me. He had a visa to travel here, and now my dad lives here, with me. I will probably have to wait three years to bring my wife. It's really hard. Right now I can't leave the country. I

have to wait for all the legalization process to end. These are really difficult situations.

The Mayan Evangelical pastor who leads a congregation on the opposite side of the city was not as fortunate as José; his mother had died five years earlier, but he could not travel home as he was not granted a travel permit from INS. He arrived alone in the United States in 1993, moved from California to Nebraska, and worked in three different meatpacking plants. He was able to bring his wife in 1996 and then his two children in 2002, all by petitioning. It is a lengthy process, possibly much longer than what the optimistic immigrants expect when they set out on their journey to El Norte.

Most of the Guatemalans know it is easier to apply for an immigrant visa by being sponsored by a family member who is a U.S. citizen or lawful permanent resident through submitting a petition to the Department of Homeland Security, DHS, to request immigrant status for the relative, or by holding an approved petition from a prospective employer. The main immigrant categories are Immediate Relative and Family Sponsored; Employment-Based; and Special Immigrants such as refugees, religious workers, or those with agreements with the U.S. government. At times the Diversity Immigrant Visa Program provides a lottery to countries with low rates of immigration to the United States, and no U.S. sponsor is required, and in 2012, 3,500 visas were granted to Guatemalans. The women seem to bypass all of this arduous paperwork in the knowledge that it would take too long and probably not be successful. As they state, those that came early on are still petitioning for family members to come, while the others opt to travel, live, and work—undocumented and unsure of their future—in the United States.

In the end, we are witnessing a recolonization of the Americas by some Central Americans who live in the grip of poverty and migrate to countries with economic opportunities, to begin earning and to continue living a life centered on family and community. With technological and transportation advances the masses have mobilized and are moving about at a much quicker pace than in the past. Ignoring this reality is no longer an option; it is across the street, in our schools and places of worship, in our local work sites, and in every facet of life in the United States. We are all here together.

And what, then, is the true definition of El Norte? If risking one's life to journey to the border and cross over to the United States results in subsistence living to provide *remesas*, remittances to family members back home, with no self-development and a constant threat of being deported or having to return home—a scenario that might separate parents from children or spouses from each other once again—what is the purpose? Possibly every situation in life has two sides—the fantasy that we imagine before we embark on any new experience, and the reality that we actually experience firsthand.

The Children Left Behind

Among the Mayan there is a generosity and concern that flows naturally across clan and kinship ties, and people rely on networking, orally transmitting information to support one another. Family alliances move beyond immediate members; everyone assists one another with cash, immigration paperwork, and the actual journey. Parents care for offspring left behind. Manuela left a child in Guatemala, and she hopes her work at the meat-packing plant will reunite them in the United States soon: "I left my two-year-old son when I came here. Now he is seven or eight years old, and he lives with my father. I tell my husband I'm going to bring my son here, where one is better off, so I can give my son everything. We talk to each other on the phone. He says he's fine, that he's in school studying. He is big now."

The extended Mayan familial network is quite far reaching and invested in the well-being of the group rather than focused on individuals. Excess and economic well-being have ironically pushed some Americans into their individualistic lifestyles, with one-fourth of them living alone; the less economically sound do not have the luxury of going it alone. They need one another, and their poverty enforces already-strong kinship ties that are cultural in origin and strengthened out of economic necessity as well as ethnic loyalty. However, these deeply entrenched families become divided across borders, connected by phone and Internet, and once the Mayan women arrive at the U.S.-Mexico border, they change clothes and lifestyles and begin the struggle to economically subsist, seeking out well-being for all those who made their journey possible.

And what about the children left behind with relatives in Guatemala? Although the Mayan women seem to feel it is not problematic for their children, those who are left behind or end up separated from their parents in the United States and in state custody do suffer the long-term effects of having been separated from their parents during their formative years. In *Across Generations*, Nancy Foner states the international dynamics in immigrant families help shape the contours and trajectories of individual lives and also have an effect outside the confines of the family, influencing the receiving communities in terms of education, labor, and local neighborhood makeup. Community members reiterated this reality in Nebraska as they try and keep up with all the needs of their changing community. Foner notes that "within an immigrant group gender, class, race, and legal status have an important impact . . . intergenerational relations are not fixed or static; they undergo shifts over time, as parents and children move through the life course into new life stages and as family and household arrangements and the very country of residence change."[11]

Recent literature and film have also taken up this topic to give the children born in transnational families a more public voice. Reyna Grande's novel *The Distance Between Us: A Memoir* deals with the physical and emotional distance she experienced when her parents went to the United States and left her in Mexico. She notes the difficulty of reconnecting once reunited, and the distance that occurs when children do arrive and assimilate into U.S. culture while the parents remain on the outskirts. Grande states the most urgent consequence of immigration is broken families and that we should all support DREAMers (undocumented youths brought to the United States as children, who now advocate for access to higher education) because they were brought over the border unbeknownst as children.[12] In the film *La Misma Luna* (*Under the Same Moon*, 2007), a young Mexican boy misses his mother so much that he decides to take off on his own and make the journey to Los Angeles to be reunited with her. Sonia Nazario's Pulitzer Prize–winning novel *Enrique's Journey* details the feelings of emotional abandonment that children suffer when their parents leave. Nazario elaborates on the resulting anger that often leads to a loss of love for parents and causes conflict once homes are reunited. In the end, the parents feel they are doing their best by providing the money for their children's survival, but the children feel money cannot fill the abysmal absence of parental closeness, especially that of a mother. When their mothers have more children in the United States, jealousy and sibling rivalry ensue, as they all push and pull for more of their parents' attention. The emotional fallout becomes most visible to those working with the recently reunited students in U.S. schools. Nazario wrote the book to give voice to the situation, and in the introduction she shares her advice with Latina mothers migrating to the United States[13] and details how the young boys journeying to find their mothers credit religious faith for their progress, praying on top of the trains, kneeling along the tracks, asking God for help and guidance.[14] In the end, faith in God is the one place where all the migrants seem to find peace and solace along this journey to survival.

A New Beginning in El Norte

The women leave more than their children behind. María laments some of the other obstacles she encountered before arriving in Nebraska:

It was a little hard when I arrived. I suffered so much. I arrived in San Diego, I didn't have a job, and my relatives didn't treat me well. It's that . . . my cousin's husband drank a lot of alcohol, and he hit her a lot. His wife is my relative, not him. Since I was defending her, he started getting angry and hating me, and then one day he hit me. It always made me so sad. I would end up crying, but then I said to myself, "Okay! Where can I find a place where I will meet normal people and find more support?" I lived there with them for three months. After that, I went to Los Angeles, and I lived in Van Nuys for two months, with relatives as well. I couldn't find a job there, but my relatives did treat me well. They gave me money if I wanted to buy something in the store, but I couldn't find a job, because if you don't have papers, you can't find a job, and so one day I just left. My other cousin lives in Omaha, Nebraska, and she called me to see if I wanted to live with her and take care of her children while she worked. Her husband came to bring me back by car, fifty-two hours in all, day and night, and that's when I arrived here in Nebraska. Here, I am no longer suffering, I am fine, and I learned a lot from the Evangelical church. I came here alone, and then I started a relationship with my husband who is Evangelical too.

Once they arrive they have to find work, and they quickly find out how difficult it is without a work permit. Often, they put off starting a relationship, tending to their crossover debt and their obligation to immediate family first. María explains why she waited to marry:

He is really good to me in every way. His relatives love me too. He wanted to know why I was suffering so much, and I told him not to be in such a hurry, that my dad and family is poor, poor. We don't even have money to buy a pair of pants so I need to help my dad because he has suffered a lot. I prefer to suffer more than my dad. He told me he could help me, and he does put forth a lot of effort. Right now, I have him, my husband. We started our relationship here. We didn't have a legal marriage because of the papers. He has papers, but I don't. He already has his residency because he has been here for eleven years, but I won't be able to solicit my papers because we have to be careful with his residency.

I told him we are poor so I am here to help my dad and my family. He understands and he lets me send money to my family whenever I want. He doesn't have any other family. His dad already died, he only has his sisters and brother, and they are all here, three sisters in California and a brother here, and they already have money. He's from a different village in Guatemala, but we speak the same language. That is, sometimes there are differences in the words, but we can understand each other. Sometimes we speak Mayan.

Forming relationships and starting a family in the United States is crucial to the Mayan women because they lived so closely with family and community in Guatemala. Manuela also mothered a child with her new partner, but paying off her debt from crossing over also took precedence over her relationship:

I arrived here, with my sister, in Nebraska, and my brother-in-law received me. Since you don't have any money when you arrive because you don't bring anything, he provided me with food, a pair of shoes, and an outfit. He paid for everything when I arrived, and later I paid him back, little by little. My boyfriend and I are still living with them. There are five of us in the house. I give him thanks for receiving us because when you arrive here, if you don't have family, who will help you, or where will you go stay, or where can you meet up with someone?

I came here on my own to be with my sister. My husband now already lived here. For about a year I was single. I told him we had to wait a while to get together or get married, because I still owed money in Guatemala and I wanted to pay it back first. He said it was fine. And then I paid back everything I owed, and my dad was really happy because they gave him back the deed to his house. If you don't pay that back it is very serious. 20,000 *quetzales* [$2,525] is a lot of money. And little by little, I paid back what

I had borrowed. Now I send more money to my dad, of course. And after that, I started a relationship with him, but we're not married in the church. He hasn't been here very long. We knew each other in Guatemala because we're from the same village. He fell in love with me when we were fifteen years old, and I . . . I wasn't attracted to him. [She laughs.]

Juana was in the most stressful situation of all of the women, as her husband feared losing his work permit and being deported.

I imagine I'm never going to be able to get my papers, ever, because it's so difficult. Faith, with faith. My other brother has a work permit, but I don't. My husband has his too, but they are most likely going to deport him because they gave him four years as soon as he applied, but then Immigration called him, and now he has to go to court. Problems. I am really worried. The lawyer says that he is going to help him, but his lawyer costs $600, and if he takes his case, he needs $1,500 more to defend the case. He doesn't have it, so he probably won't, because it is so much money. What's going to happen if they deport him, or if they arrest him? It is a very serious situation.

Now I would like my daughters to come, someday, but not right now, because of this problem. God willing, someday, they will. Or maybe we will go back again, for my daughters, so we can all live there. For the children it's very different here, they have everything, but in Guatemala there isn't food, water, or milk, or any money, and you just die. You need dollars so you can afford raising your children. I don't know what I am going to do if they deport my husband, oh my God, I hope they don't. If they deport him, maybe we all will go. If they deport him, I think maybe I have nothing. How will I take care of the children, how will I take care of them? I know, I can, but it's better when they're with their father.

Increased enforcement of immigration policies has affected many families. They fear it because it separates many spouses and many parents from their children. Considering numbers alone, the U.S. Immigration and Customs Enforcement, ICE, reports that some 397,000 undocumented immigrants were deported in 2011 and 410,000 in 2012. Other sources report there have been a record two million deportations thus far during the Obama administration. Further analysis of these numbers indicates some caution is needed because of changing definitions of immigration policy in different presidential administrations. For example, prior to 1996, immigration policy distinguished between immigrants who were "excluded" or stopped from entering U.S. territory and those who were "deported" after they had made their way into the United States, but since then exclusion and deportation have been considered a single procedure called "removal."[15] This administrative decision complicates analyzing and assessing historical deportation numbers and trends. One study of these numbers indicates that "traditional deportations" have fallen steadily since the advent of the Obama administration, perhaps by as much as 40 percent. However, critics of current immigration policies advocate that presidents stop deporting undocumented immigrants with close family ties in the United States and those who have no criminal history other than immigration-related violations.[16] On the point of criminal histories, ICE reports that in a recent year (2013), 59 percent of all those deported had committed crimes not related to immigration. And the countries of origin of such deportees were, in numerical order: Mexico, Guatemala, Honduras, and El Salvador.

An especially delicate question involves the treatment of American-born minor children of those immigrants who are expelled from the United States. Given the poorly coordinated child welfare policies of any number of relevant federal agencies, an early study concluded that some 5,000 minors during a six-month period were left in such a predicament after their parent(s) were deported or detained for legal proceedings.[17] One study states that parents seeking economic security come to the United States, but are losing custody of their children when they fail to respect American social service system regulations, although they believe they are parenting well.[18] Of the more than two million people deported between 1998 and 2003, only 8 percent were parents. However, in the first half of 2011, 22 percent of deportees were parents.

Most of the Mayan women interviewed in this study cannot marry legally in the United States, because they are undocumented. This causes a number of challenging legal, social, and personal crises given their backgrounds. For example, María and her husband followed Mayan familial traditions when they decided to marry. He would have to contact her father in Guatemala before any marriage could take place, so his family went to hers to ask permission. Love overcomes all, and they forge on as a married couple without the official paperwork. She has moved into the in-laws' home with him, much as she would have done in Guatemala. Martha points out that María was following Mayan tradition and practices, possibly without even realizing or knowing them, and the others do the same. They do not have labels and names for their Mayan cultural practices and beliefs; it is simply their innate way of life, the way they have always followed family traditions and practices as Mayans.

In asking the Mayan women about their lives I see that they don't have the luxury of questioning their life events much. They are surviving, day to day, month to month, and they aren't planning ahead. They have dreams for their future, but they stop at their present need for food and shelter for their immediate and extended family because so much of their future is unsure. They live exiled, unable to return home because they lack documentation and the border crossing is perilous, and unable to put down firm roots in their new country, again because they lack documentation and also fear being deported and losing any economic gain they've accrued. They never know where they will end up or if their bicultural families will be divided or separated. They have an immense fear that La Migra, or ICE, will show up again, unannounced, for a raid at their job sites or homes, putting their worst-case scenario into play once more.

Regardless of all the contradiction and controversy, the Mayan women immigrants operate with unbridled optimism. Somehow, even among all the discrimination, poverty, and roadblocks they experience, they maintain the hope that one day they will be treated as equals, and they will have an equal right to work with dignity for economic gain in whatever place presently provides labor opportunities.

This grueling journey they make, through unknown terrain, with unknown fellow travelers and with no turning back, is simply what they choose to do to survive. There's no way to map their journey as they don't even know the names of the places where they crossed the border, nor whom their guides were. It was just a blind journey, being led by *coyotes*, entrusting self to chance. It is a journey to survival.

In their new homeland, the immigrants struggle to find meaning and build the best life possible. The definition of family in this century is undergoing tremendous change as it is stretched by global migrations and the limitations on immigrants. Starting new families in new countries, and supporting children left with relatives in another country, is a new way of life for immigrants. These are transnational families, with single members of kinship clans moving beyond borders, and the distances often cause family disintegration. José comments on the devastating effects of immigration on family, and how he has found solace weaving his way through his past and present:

> Maybe what has really helped me has been to seek out God, each day, because with God one feels the way of the good. I have been trying to support the priest, to help him in everything, and that has helped me so much, to stay faithful to my family and to keep moving forward each day. There are a lot of people who start a second family here. It's hard, it's really hard. Just yesterday I received a letter from my wife. Now they are so sad, they suffer so much, they want to be with me, and I say, be faithful, and remain faithful to my home, and I listen to my family and tell myself my behavior

has helped them feel the way they do, and helped them express themselves with me the way they do. My wife has been fine in our town. She has the house, she is nearby one of my brothers, and there are other brothers-in-law, and her brothers are nearby, and they have her safe. But now, when I got to Guatemala, I realize, a woman who stays there alone, and stays faithful. . . . It's very difficult. The majority can't do it. I have seen a large percentage of homes end up destroyed. I have noticed a situation that I discovered here: a Hispanic that has never had an opportunity to have money in their hands thinks that with money, with dollars, he is going to encounter so many things. They start thinking about having power and possessions. They buy this, they buy that, they buy a car, they look for another woman, and they end up destroying themselves. There are husbands that don't return in the end, and there are women who come to work and don't go back again. And that happens a lot among Hispanics.

For me, there is nothing greater than when one finds the purpose of their life. And I say this because after what I suffered in the army, after being so close to *chewing* death, I felt I was already dead. When they hit me in the stomach and I vomited blood, I felt that's it, I felt *la muerte*, death. And then, years later, when I was going to get out of the army, my nervous system was failing, and I had ended up in such a terrible situation, about to die, and I discovered there is a God, a God that loves me, a faithful God that is leading me down a path. That's when I found the purpose of my life. And I understood that I have to take care of my life, that the older I am getting, the more I should love my life, the more I should take care of myself in what I am going to eat and how I am going to live. Each day I try to have a better life and to have a better relationship with God. God is never going to abandon me, or be unfaithful to me.

As can be seen here, the Guatemalans whose interviews make up this book are extremely religious people with a deep spiritual practice centered on faith and a dedication to family. They also work under duress in the United States to support their extended Guatemalan families, some of them struggling to ensure greed doesn't sway their morals or values. Religion is at the center of their new lives, and the next chapter details their religious practice and changing lifestyles in their new homeland.

4

Religious Practice and
Community Life in Nebraska

I pull off the main highway and drive through the city, noting the buzzing activity at the Casey's General Store and the local McDonald's. There is a silence and ease in these Nebraska communities, with their motels and diners, small seed stores, secondhand shops, and dollar stores interspersed between Hispanic food and supply stores with names like "El Quetzal," the Guatemalan national bird, and "El Charro," a Mexican cowboy. All the typical retailers are here, as well as Valentino's Pizzeria, a Nebraska landmark. Mexican and Salvadoran restaurants display a multicultural flavor. There are businesses and recreational facilities offering their services in Spanish on bilingual signage. The overabundance of places of worship is another sign of the new arrivals.

Juana agreed to meet me on a snowy, freezing day in 2005. It was a typical wintery day, travel advisories warning below-zero windchill temperatures and snow. I wondered how the Mayans from Guatemala, where temperatures are between seventy and eighty degrees during the day, and in the highlands dip down into the forties at night, can weather these winters, but they seem to be amazingly adaptive people.

Juana is late so I wait in the cold church. I remember being inside a Guatemalan Catholic church built upon Mayan ruins, next to the colorful Chichicastenango market that attracts tourists from all over the world. I watched small Mayans enter silently and humbly. They crouched down low in both the center and side aisles, murmuring prayers and lining up their blue, white, black, red, and yellow candles on the floor of the church, lighting them, and continuing to hover down near the ground, deep in prayer. They never went near the saints' statues or the front of the church. The rites they came to practice were altogether different and conducted in the center and side aisles. When I shared this later with Native American colleagues they excitedly assured me this happens in the U.S. Southwest too, where Native Americans are invited to carry out their rites within the Catholic church as well.

This church where I now sit is Catholic, and the Spanish masses are a way the church invites Latinos to come worship in their language; one Catholic church in Omaha even offers a mass in a Mayan language. Places of worship are one place where the Mayans feel welcome, and they therefore come often. Juana has asked to meet me here, not at her house. It's neutral ground, and it's the place where we met each other for the first time, after Spanish mass.

Juana is a woman of few words. She sits for a second, getting adjusted, and says, "The car wouldn't start." [Silence.] "I thought it wasn't going to start, but it did." Juana is so solid. I observe her and suddenly see something that baffles me. In this ten-degree weather she is wearing flip-flops. I exclaim, "Juana, you're wearing sandals in this weather?! Aren't your feet *freezing*?" She glances down at her flip-flops and then just shrugs her shoulders. "I forgot to put my shoes on when I left the house." I tell her I am really concerned, that in Nebraska she needs to wear shoes and socks or she will get sick! She is unmoved and just smiles. She eventually repeats that she left home really fast, because she wanted to make it here, and she forgot to change shoes. She is also wearing a thin little jacket and a T-shirt, and nothing more. It is really cold in the church. I have brought a long, black wool coat, and I ask her if she wants to put it on. She refuses initially, saying she's all right, but I keep insisting, and in the end she lets me drape it all around her, tucking it in, and now she is really smiling. I wonder when the last time was that someone mothered her like this, she being quite the mother herself, having four children divided between the United States and Guatemala. When I tell Martha about how Juana endured the harsh winter, she says these are some of the most weathered people on earth and that they are extremely well equipped for survival, adding, "A lot of Indians never even had shoes, Anna."

Excerpts from my conversation with Juana are sprinkled throughout these chapters. Juana always seems to be deciphering her next move or question when you talk to her because she is constantly decoding three languages and cultures, two of which she hasn't yet mastered. However, of all the women, she is the one who assuredly asked me the most questions about myself and my personal life. When we had finished talking I offered to take her home, and she agreed. I told her I was worried about her feet getting cold, so I was going to warm the car up and then come in to get her.

When I step back inside the side door of the church I see a vision that is still branded in my mind. Juana is on her knees in the center aisle, on the very axis of the empty church, crouched low, praying to her God, asking for all the things she has told me she is so concerned about. I slink into my comfort-zone pew where I began my journey into these women's lives so long ago, recalling the day I stepped up from this same place to ask them to let me enter into their worlds. They have related their stories to me, without asking for anything in return. Now I try to imagine being her and ask myself what it is like. I sit silently with her, hoping that everything she is praying for will be, just as she needs it to be. I wonder if she has ever had the luxury of being alone in this church, and therefore able to offer up a Mayan-style prayer, in the center aisle, down low on her knees. I now understand what she was thinking when she agreed for me to leave her alone for a few minutes.

Later, Martha explains they don't recognize their traditions as "Mayan" because Mayan spirituality has been denigrated and actively suppressed since colonization. The conquistadors went to great lengths to erase any signs of Mayan spirituality, rituals, and beliefs, substituting them with Catholic ones. The women say they are Catholic, or Evangelical.

Mayan Spirituality and Religion in Guatemala

Martha naturally displays Mayan spiritual practices as well. Before presenting at a conference together we discussed whether she would feel comfortable wearing her *traje* in a planned fashion show, and she decided she would not be, as it didn't feel like something she wanted to put on display or model as extraordinary or exquisite because it is an integral part of her identity. However, she was dressed so strikingly that the organizers persuaded her to display it, and she did. Without any ostentation she cupped her hands near her heart and blew across them, dispersing all the love she embodies, handing it over and spreading it out to all the Latinas there. When I asked her what the meaning of that display was, she said it was a way to spread peace, as in giving a blessing to the others. Calixta Gabriel Xiquín further explains this practice: "We don't even have a word like religion in our language. For us it is life itself: respect, dignity, love for one's neighbor. All these things are the presence of God. One way the Maya prays is by blowing 'huh' into one's hand . . . before a man cuts down a tree, he asks permission from the earth by saying 'huh' because the earth is his mother. My parents taught me this prayer, and even now I do this prayer for many things. But it doesn't translate well because it doesn't have words. It comes from the heart."[1] Martha thus shared her Mayan spirituality with those in attendance in a nonverbal way; she can't communicate with them in English, nor in Q'anjob'al, her Mayan language, and although she speaks Spanish, some of them don't. Mayan spiritual practices such as this exude from the women organically.

The Mayan women's different ways of worshipping traverse the border with them. María states she is Evangelical, not Catholic. Juana explains: "At home we didn't really practice Mayan rites. My parents and my maternal grandparents were Catholics, and my paternal grandparents were Evangelical. I have always been

Catholic, from the beginning. They baptized me, and I made my First Communion."

Guatemala exhibits the blending of Mayan, African, and European religious beliefs and practices. These synchronistic celebrations of Catholicism in Latin America were the norm for over five centuries, but changing times have ushered in new religious movements. The Mayan women appear to be quite comfortable exploring the best fit in terms of religion. Guatemalan religious history has had many phases: the Spanish conquest's attempt to convert the Mayans, the ouster of Catholic religious orders, the arrival of Protestants, the Catholic catechist movement that eroded the Mayan ancestral practice of *costumbre* and the religious divisions that ensued, the Catholic Church's focus on community development after Vatican II, and the government's attack on social and community-based projects that caused many to convert to Protestantism to avoid this violence.[2] Throughout the process Mayans have not lost their spirituality; at times it goes undercover, but it has always been present.

Zur points out that in the mid-1950s Acción Católica, Catholic Action, organized Spanish-language catechist classes through which Mayans were introduced not only to orthodox Catholicism but to a new understanding of their social, economic, and political position within the Guatemalan state.[3] This movement challenged the existing structure of Mayan communities and led to the rejection of *costumbre*, or "Custom," which was composed of hierarchal brotherhoods led by elders. The movement's adherents named and trained catechists who were instructed to teach their communities about the "new" Catholicism.

During the armed conflict any religious or educational institutions suspected of empowering the indigenous or leading them into insurrection were targeted. "Particularly subject to lethal attack were costumbrista diviners (*zajorines*/aj q'ij); it was believed that they were using their powers to protect the guerrillas."[4] The armed conflict shattered religious and community bonds as people fled from the violence, often taking refuge in Protestantism as the least suspect of the various religions during that time period. Prior to the coup, some indigenous people had already begun practicing Protestantism and "new" Catholicism.

Vicente, the Mayan Evangelical pastor now living in Nebraska, stated the *guerrilla* was organized from within the Catholic Church and that violent acts are prohibited for Evangelicals because they contradict the teachings in the Bible. He also spoke out strongly against Mayan *costumbre*, stating it is "satanic worship." Martha says his attitude is understandable:

> Since the conquest, the Mayan spiritual belief system has been depicted as something highly negative, blasphemous, and sinful, in an effort to transfer worship over to Catholicism. My grandfather was a catechist and my parents attended the Maryknoll school. I recall hearing how the priests gathered the day keepers and healers and took away their sacred objects and divination materials, throwing them over mountainsides, an action mirroring those of the conquest five hundred years earlier. The resulting hysterical tears they cried in anguish were unbearable to observers. The elders wept without solace, as if they had taken a child from them and killed it before their eyes.

Some Mayans ended up feeling alienated from their rituals and religious practices that were prohibited.

In the 1970s and 1980s liberation theology emerged from within the Catholic Church and was pivotal in the Central American wars. The doctrine mobilized some peasants, who then joined the revolutionary movements to fight against poverty. According to the CEH report, this alliance with the *guerrilla* made the church suspect, and many catechists, priests, nuns, and missionaries were victims of the violence, giving their lives as testimony of the cruelty of the armed conflict.[5] With the fall of the Left in Latin America, the movement has lost popularity, but still exists. "Liberation theology today tends to be very much focused on family and social issues, concerning itself with things like alcoholism, domestic abuse, poverty alleviation and things of that nature."[6]

RELIGIOUS PRACTICE AND COMMUNITY LIFE

The indigenous movements across the Americas that occurred in the 1990s were partially a result of being asked to celebrate the five-hundred-year anniversary of their "discovery." At that time indigenous peoples began meeting across borders and countries, sharing their histories and their lives and pondering the world order and the political and economic processes that had put them in their present-day situation, while analyzing their future as well. Many began reclaiming and valuing the cultural practices and sacred places that had been stripped from them in an effort to convert them to Catholicism. Catechists called on day keepers for reconciliation, thus lifting the ban and negativity associated with Mayan spiritual practices of *costumbre*.[7] Molesky-Poz points out this is not a Mayan revival movement but the result of support from church parishes, historical reconciliation, and cultural recuperation in each village that has allowed Mayans to come forth and say they still practice Maya belief and ritual, but now without fear of repercussions.[8]

The most widely practiced religion in Latin America since the conquest is still Catholicism, although religious pluralism has increased over the past two decades. In the 1970s and 1980s, in the aftermath of armed conflicts, a Latin American Protestant revival arose in competition with Catholicism. Guatemala is now one-third Protestant, and 12 percent of all Latin Americans practice Protestantism. General Ríos Montt rose to power in 1982, and the way he shared his Christian religious practice with the public and believed he was led by God in governing the country attracted some of the approximately two million new Protestant converts.

The Mayan women understand that different religions are just separate ways of praising God, but religiosity has had a pivotal position in their country's history, as they have directly experienced. Attempts have been made to pass laws protecting the Mayans and their rights, but the laws were not enacted. "Despite the 1996 agreement to promote indigenous cultural and social rights, the free expression of Mayan religion, language, and other facets of identity continues to be hampered by a shortage of resources and a lack of political will to enforce laws and implement the 1996 peace accords."[9]

Mayan Religious Practice, Family Dynamics, and Consumerism in Nebraska

For many of the immigrants their religious practice is the place where they feel a true sense of community similar to that in Guatemala. Father Matthew, a Catholic priest in one town, states that community ceremonies enliven spirituality even more than Sunday mass attendance. Early on, Martha spoke to me about the need to orient her American parish priest at another Catholic church, saying he just didn't comprehend the church's social justice role. It may be that the priest rejects it, hasn't lived abroad, or hasn't been indoctrinated that way in the U.S. seminary, or perhaps the dioceses give instructions in order to ensure that the Catholic Church stays within apolitical parameters. Due to their experiences in Guatemala, the Mayan immigrants' view of the church's role is different. However, this priest they aimed to change was the person who helped José secure a visa to return for his mother's death, and the same priest later promoted a march against anti-immigrant legislation from the pulpit and also recommended Martha's husband attend prayer sessions with prisoners in the local jail.

Another way Guatemalan Mayan immigrants are changing parts of Catholicism in the United States is through the creation of programs such as Pastoral Maya, a national organization that provides "pastoral care in the indigenous languages of Maya Catholics living and serving in more than thirty Catholic communities in the United States. The ministry emphasizes Maya lay Catholic pastoral leadership formation, the development of national level communication linkages via a website, the initiation of Maya youth ministry, and the transmission of Maya cultural values and traditions among families, especially children. Pastoral Maya works in collaboration with parishes and dioceses including Omaha, as well as institutions and organizations that share the goal of assisting Maya families in living their faith fully and facilitating the integration of their families into the American church and society."[10] One of the fruits of their labor occurred at a recent All Nations Powwow; the Native Americans welcomed the Mayans as Natives of the Americas, a reception the Maya appreciated, knowing there is more strength in unity.

There are separate allegiances regarding faith and belief among the Mayan women in Nebraska, but the one common denominator is a strong devotion to being a good person, free of vice, who nurtures the family unit above all; this lies at the center of their religious practice. Both Father Matthew and Pastor Vicente spoke of their cooperation with their followers to respect and support the family unit above all.

Vicente came to Nebraska to work in the meatpacking plants, but in 2000 he started a church in a garage, to combat violence and drug abuse. He says he is there to help the community spiritually, so they can rise above difficult moments in their lives. He states his religion is for the poor, and adds, "The rich don't need God. Their God is money." Today they have a beautiful structure with an excellent sound system, but he dreams of a larger place of worship to house a refuge for drug addicts. He is especially concerned about the women who arrive alone, many having suffered violence on the journey. He frets for the safety of the undocumented once they have arrived; they may be stopped and asked for driver's licenses that they don't have, and if that is the case they are then arrested, leaving children parentless, thus creating more family disintegration.

As José pointed out, there is much family disintegration among the immigrants. Manuela has started a family with Guillermo, knowing he has a wife and family back in Guatemala. Many immigrants in the United States are in this same situation; going it alone gets lonely. In Nebraska, María converted to Evangelicalism to join her husband and his family in marriage. Manuela's family converted from Catholicism to Evangelicalism while still in Guatemala, but she has been open to practicing different religions within her relationship, as long as there is no alcohol abuse:

> I'm Christian, but then I met Guillermo and he was Catholic. When I saw he doesn't drink every day and that he goes to church I told him it was fine. I've seen a coworker whose husband drinks a lot, and, oh my, you should have seen her. She came to work really badly beaten up. Her one eye was almost closed, and the other was really black. And since there are a lot of us working together we told her, "You have to call the police if your husband hits you! You have to deport him!" But *ay*, she didn't do it. He was drunk, and on everything, but she didn't call them.

For some of the Mayan women, tolerating abuse starts in the home. There are set gender roles for domestic work among Mayans in Guatemala, but all of that changes when the women enter the workforce here with men. There are also laws and rulings that prohibit physical violations. They may not speak English very well, but they know this. Now they adapt to these protections. The local sheriff was impressed with how quickly the Mayans have learned this and stated that they are helpful, cooperative, and work to help defend these laws. They know they can have abusive husbands deported and then apply for citizenship. Federal law provides numerous forms of protection for immigrant women, granting "U" visas for victims of crime and "T" visas for victims of severe forms of trafficking, and under the Violence Against Women Act, VAWA, allowing for "self-petitioning."[11] The sheriff says some men also report they have been abused and want their wives deported, thus setting their own citizenship application in process.

Knowledge of these U.S. policies assures Manuela she will not have to suffer abuse from an alcoholic as her coworker and mother did, and she asserted this to her mate before she married him. She explains:

> I'm not Catholic, I'm Christian, because of my dad. They baptized me in the Catholic Church, but then later, they went to the other

church because in Guatemala the Catholics drink a lot. When they organize the *fiesta*, a religious celebration, they get really drunk. Here it's different. It's really calm, and they are so respectful.

My dad became a Christian because he was an alcoholic. He drank too much, and then he would hit my mom. She suffered a lot when he was like that, so they went to the Christian church because they don't give you wine, and they don't allow drinking. They have lectures. In the Catholic Church it's your preference if you want to drink or not. I have an uncle who died from drinking, because of his liver. He couldn't stop. He used to steal things from my grandpa to buy that. At that point it's an illness.

Manuela believes Catholicism encourages and condones alcoholism. I shared this with Father Matthew, and he agreed that unfortunately some people abuse alcohol, but that it has always been a part of the sacred mass, and his male church parishioners focus on socializing without drinking, on being faithful to their partners, and striving to be good family men. He feels poverty and loneliness contribute to alcohol abuse, which in turn causes family problems. He asks his fold to be proper in the Lord and proper within the family.

Alcohol consumption is forbidden for Evangelicals here and in Guatemala. Pastor Vicente states they work with alcoholics and drug addicts, helping them find work and, if need be, trying to save matrimonies. He notes, "The Gospel changed things. Drinking is not allowed, nor is having two women or two men." In his opinion, alcohol provokes violence: "If your mother is cooking, but your father is going to arrive drunk and hit her, nothing changes." Personally, he changed by reading the Gospel, and then his entire family joined him in his newfound Evangelical faith and everything changed. He assures, "With alcohol, there's no change. Without it, there is peace." Pastor Vicente states his congregation attempts to avoid sin at all costs, but they realize it is very difficult.

There are not accurate measures of Guatemalan male alcohol

abuse, but it is interesting to note that of the six Mayan women interviewed, four have been victimized or otherwise affected because of alcoholism in their immediate or extended families. A World Health Organization 2011 report states that although 84.7 percent of women and 49.4 percent of men in Guatemala are life-time abstainers from alcohol, in 2004 liver cirrhosis accounted for 60.8 percent of deaths among men and 21.2 percent among women.

Depending on their past familial experiences, the women settle into their personal religious practice and begin setting up a new household and life. Their U.S. experience can have both positive and negative qualities for the Mayan women. Martha expresses how difficult the transition was for her:

> When I came to the U.S. I was very disappointed, due to the drastic change in my activities. In Guatemala I dealt with a lot of people, ministers, institutions, and organizations, researching and preparing reports, and I liked going from place to place a lot. A professional man or woman arrives home and rests, because they have servants. When I came here, both men and women can have a paying job, and therefore they share the responsibil-ities in the household.

> The first days I would get so tired because all of a sudden I had to work a lot, but at home. I didn't understand the news, or what was happening. Not knowing anyone, after having gone to meetings back to back was difficult. You can walk outside, down the street, but you don't know the people, there isn't any infor-mation in Spanish, and you don't have anything to do with other people. It was very different. Here, making the food and staying home as a housewife is very difficult.

> I do go to church. I am the vice-president of the Hispanic Pas-toral Counsel. I have started doing what I like to do: working with people. There are organizations in which I would like to partici-pate, such as in the town meetings, but everything is in English. I had my children after I came here, and after my first son was

born I couldn't go to the library or English classes at the meat-packing plant anymore.

The women have to confront many changes once they arrive. They often feel alone and isolated, and these women note the strength that comes from living in multigenerational families in which everyone does their part and keeps the household running. Martha sadly tells me her children don't have aunts, uncles, or other family members in their Nebraska city. She remembers running through the streets of her Guatemalan town to go and visit an aunt or uncle on her own, and she laments her children's physical distance from their relatives.

Food purchase and preparation is a daunting task in the beginning as well, because everything is unknown. Martha explains, "We have worked together to figure out how to prepare the food. Over there we eat vegetables, and here there is more meat. Sometimes, since you don't know how to make it, or you aren't familiar with the vegetables here, you don't eat right." The women were appreciative that the government provided cooking classes to teach them how to prepare available foods and create healthy menus for their families. Juana likes the food in the United States because it is more filling than herbs, there's a lot of variety, and there's Mexican food. María confesses she feels embarrassed to eat in local restaurants because there are only Americans there. She imagines they don't mind and notes that the men enter, but she feels uncomfortable going out to eat in her new city.

Martha is concerned how U.S. capitalism and consumerism changes immigrants, pondering: "And how do we bring up our children in a consumer society? What will the future values be?" Lucía notes that achieving the U.S. level of consumerism and obtaining health insurance are what force them to constantly increase their earnings and purchasing power: "Thank God, I now have my papers and insurance, but if you get ill, as I did, the amount they take out of your paycheck doesn't cover it all. I had a migraine and I got a bill for $1,600, and the insurance paid $1,000 and I have to pay $600." Lucía is trying to send money to her sons and keep up with her medical bills and also with the higher cost of living in the United States: "I worry about bills here in this country, because there in Guatemala you live in poverty but you don't pay electricity and other bills. There you can buy a candle, and you don't pay cable. You are poor. We don't have television, we don't have water. [She laughs.] And here you do. [She points at all the things in the house.] Look!"

Lucía is using the insurance benefits that go along with her job at the meatpacking plant, but Martha points out that medical systems and preventative care are all new for the Mayans:

> We are not accustomed to medical checkups. We usually go to the doctor when we are about to die. There is no prevention, because there were never any resources, not even for emergencies, so when the women arrive here they aren't used to going in for checkups to prevent problems, but it's because of a lack of information. Health care is so important. Women, Infants, and Children Program, wic, provides checkups and prevention. If they are made aware, they take the precautions, and the children in the wic program are healthier, but not all children qualify for it. Unfortunately, often the women won't take the prenatal medications or multivitamins because in general there is mistrust about Western medicine.

Some of the fear of the vitamins may linger from being given "vitamins" by the *coyotes* to enhance energy while making the border crossing. Their new terrain is unchartered territory.

Martha mulls over the way migration affects Guatemala as well. As the Mayan men and women move between two countries, taking material goods, social practices, customs, and a third language, it transforms both societies. Martha says the children with good tennis shoes and nice school supplies have parents working in the United States, and the towns with nice churches, plazas, and schools are usually receiving financial assistance from the Mayans who now live abroad. José points out that while living in a consumer society many Mayans don't easily forget home, pouring vast amounts of their limited income into the beloved towns they one day hope to return to, with their pockets full this time, and their towns now enhanced due to their investments. José lives with others so that he can send home as much money as possible: "I live with five Guatemalans, in a big house, with two bathrooms, and we work opposite shifts, so there are never more than two or three in the house at a time during the day. I send half of my paycheck home to my family in Guatemala." Lucía's efforts in the United States are to support her children in Guatemala as well: "My son likes school a lot. He told me he needs a computer because he wants to learn how to use it, and I told him I'm going to give him whatever I can."

Manuela dreams of having a house in the future, for her children, but there was no talk of her own education or personal betterment. She says:

I like it here in Nebraska. We are probably going to stop paying rent and buy a house for when the kids grow up. I tell my husband we need to plan and decide if we are going to build a house here or in Guatemala. He already has a house with his father and his mother, and with his family, because he has a wife and a son, so I told him we probably have to build another house. He is going to decide, but I don't know [she laughs], because now I am with him and he's going to decide where he's going and that's where I'm going.

The way that Manuela relinquishes important decision making to her husband exemplifies traditional Mayan gender roles. Father Matthew notes this among the Mayan women as well, stating they seem more dependent on the men and usually will not stand up to them, even if they are abusing alcohol.

Lucía seems content to stay in her new life in Nebraska: "I asked God if I could have a job, a good life, and thank God, now, I have made a joyful life with my husband, and he treats me very well. That is the biggest happiness I have now." Juana ponders between putting down roots here or going back home, having children in each country. But in the end the standard of living in Nebraska seems a better choice for her children's well-being, so she hopes to bring her two children in Guatemala to the United States.

María has also decided she feels at home in her new land:

> I think this American society is very beautiful. Sometimes I want to get married and have a house that will be mine, but if they end up taking our papers away, we don't know what would happen to the house, so the best thing we can do is save and fight for our families' well-being. We both want to see our parents again, before they die, but I think about how difficult crossing the border is, and I don't ever want to go through that again because I suffered so much there. Here it is so beautiful, but if one day Immigration takes us out? Our life isn't very secure. We never know what is going to happen. And in the end, it's better that I am here to send them the money that I can earn here because if I go back to Guatemala I am not going to work. I prefer to be here and see what day God is going to take me out of here.

The Mayan women plan on staying, but for some of them, their undocumented status really doesn't allow for any future security or investments. In the meantime, they enjoy the modern comforts and commodities in their rented homes, as well as their purchasing power at the supermarkets and in restaurants.

José feels appreciative and at home here, and he is invested in community building:

> A Peruvian friend and I are organizing a Hispanic pastoral counsel, and planning various activities for here in the community. Tomorrow there's a meeting with the mayor, to talk about cleaning, organizing, and city control projects. In January we had a very beautiful festival here, for Americans and Hispanics. We did dances and everything cultural from all of our countries, and they really liked it a lot. That's how we have been trying to build relationships, with the little bit of English I know, we are getting to know each other, by eating together at church.

Here, in this city, there isn't any violent crime. This is a really peaceful place. It's ideal. I like my weekly routine, going to work and to church, and helping my parish priest. We teach catechism to the children, and we are here helping the readers, and it's really calm. Here you never hear of people robbing, not at all.

The Mayans interviewed appreciate the safety in their small town and expressed their gratitude that the meatpacking plants provide their wages in a timely fashion, knowing some undocumented workers are cheated out of their wages due to the difficulty in pressing charges for such offenses. They have come here to work, and they want to stay for now.

Local Community Agencies and Intercultural Communication

The immigrants work diligently to meet the demands of their new American lifestyle, and their presence in Nebraska cities affects local support service agencies. Educators, social service providers, religious leaders, and law authorities all express concern for the family unit and communication between parents and children. Father Matthew comments that the immigrants' biggest challenge is communication. He outlines the difficulties within intergenerational communication: the parents speak Mayan languages, everyone speaks Spanish at the church, the children and grandchildren speak English only and don't like to speak their Mayan languages. Father Matthew gives sermons in Spanish, and if needed they translate them to English simultaneously, or he gives a synopsis in English for the youth. The Mayans in his city go to the Spanish masses, and they are crowded. He is encouraging parents to go to mass in English as the children understand that language better, and it will integrate them with the other parishioners. They do have bilingual events, but there is usually a smaller percentage of English speakers that attend.

There is a language disconnect between parents and children, and between schools and the community, that divides families.

He admires the way the schools are trying to bridge the gap with a learning resource center, which is open evenings and houses computers, where students and parents can come and receive help with homework and computer skills, and he adds it is well visited. His main concern is the fact that young people living between three languages and cultures can't express their emotions to parents due to language barriers. They end up listening to pop music and bonding with other youth, searching for what's "cool" or "adult." Both he and the parents fear when teenagers are stepping out of family and church activities to spend time using the computer.

The superintendent also points out that language is a barrier, and often the parents bring their children as an interpreter, and he states, "This is good for kids, to be bilingual." On the other side of town the sheriff feels it is sad when a child interprets for parents, possibly because the topic is sensitive and might deal with issues that the child really shouldn't hear about. He likes seeing kids come up through the school system and then start working in local service offices using their bilingual skills. He says 99 percent of the immigrants are law-abiding citizens, but his main concerns are gang recruitment and drug trafficking; his goal is to protect all children under his jurisdiction. In his department they have had to start speaking Spanish, and he says the Nebraska Law Enforcement training is going to start including two weeks of Spanish instruction. They have bilingual employees at the sheriff's department and are in the process of hiring a bilingual deputy. He appreciates the way the immigrants will help out, such as translating for him, but there is a lack of interpreters to serve the schools, court, and hospitals. For example, one man needed a K'iche' interpreter in county court; those interpreters come from a nearby larger city, and the court system pays their fees and mileage. Language issues have moved from bilingual to multilingual in this meatpacking city.

While interviewing Lucía I was shocked when the police arrived at her home, but she was unaffected; she called to her husband, and he talked to them. She informed me they were looking for a person and that her husband helps them in any way he can, because he speaks English well. She consoled, "They are just doing their job. We always help them if we can." The sheriff stated this as well. He spoke to the fact that in each different immigrant community they pinpoint the leaders of the group and communicate with the new arrivals through that spokesperson, in a clan-to-clan style of interaction. In this way local law authorities respect the centuries-old Mayan community leadership structures with elders as honored leaders. The sheriff was very pleased to tell me the Guatemalan Mayans trust him and his employees, unlike in their home countries.

The Mayan women also pinpoint communication as the major challenge in their new land. María details how it divides:

> There are a lot of Mayan languages in Guatemala and we all speak different ones, and some of us don't speak much Spanish. Even though I live here, I still feel Mayan. I have an indigenous Mayan work mate from Quetzaltenango, but when I asked her to speak *dialecto* she denied knowing it. I asked her why she was ashamed to speak it, and she asked how I knew she spoke *dialecto*. I told her I notice Ladino people don't have an accent from their *dialecto*, but indigenous people do, and sometimes they say words that aren't from Spanish. I told her I missed speaking *dialecto*, and she admitted she speaks it too. I told her, "I do speak *dialecto*. I am not ashamed to say it. If a person asks me if I am indigenous I am going to say the truth, that I am a Mayan from there." That attitude, that practice of denying you speak *dialecto* comes from Guatemala. I am not ashamed of it. I like speaking the *dialecto* from there, if I'm with another person that speaks *dialecto*.
>
> Here, with the Americans, it's as if we don't speak Spanish back home. It's as if they talk to you and you don't understand what they are saying, and you stay quiet, because you don't know what they are talking about. You are just looking at the other person.

I studied English for a month, last year, but I didn't retain anything. [She laughs.] My husband does know how to speak English because he went to classes at work. We want to go to college, and when I go back to Guatemala I would like to know English. The problem is I work at night so first I need to learn how to drive, but I'm afraid because it was so dangerous to drive in Guatemala.

There is so much new terrain for immigrants to conquer: the language, work, and driving. They identify their barriers, but continue forward with optimism. Language slows Juana down into a snail-like pace as she grapples for words between her three inventories. She verbalizes how she has been tongue-tied in the United States, and at one of the women's meetings she breaks down and cries while telling about the humiliation of being ridiculed at the meatpacking plant by Mexicans who speak Spanish well:

Here, I learned all the Spanish I know, at work. But I want to learn to speak really well because when I started working here I was afraid. All of a sudden I started talking so softly. I just couldn't talk. But in my *dialecto*, my language, I *do* have my voice [she laughs], but in Spanish . . . it's because I can't. When I started working here when I arrived five years ago, I couldn't speak English either. I was afraid to talk. It was just that I couldn't speak correctly. Sometimes, the Mexican women, since they speak Spanish only, they made fun of me because I couldn't speak it. They don't speak Mayan languages, or they speak them very little, or not at all. The Mexican women always laugh at us because we don't know Spanish. Sometimes it's easier to just be silent than to be humiliated.

Juana is living mutely most of the time, but she so wants to have a voice and presence on the job and in her new homeland. She manages to take all this gatekeeping, marginalization, and linguistic discrimination in stride.

Lucía also feels uncomfortable when she can't hold her own in English, and she wonders what a real conversation with Americans would be like:

I've been here in Nebraska for about six years. I already knew Spanish when I arrived here, but the truth is, you need to know a lot of English to speak with the Americans. So we just talk to them a little bit, but we stay apart because we don't speak much. I can't figure out what's going on, and I can't ask them because I don't speak English. Here it is so different. I think maybe the people who live here don't know what there is outside of here. I guess they think they can't talk to someone who doesn't know English, so then they are just like us. It's as if we are afraid to talk to each other because we can't speak each other's language. What are we going to say to them? Some of them are really good, good people. I have seen them talk to us. They talk to us in English with good intentions. Americans have good hearts too. There are Americans who work in the plant too, and there they talk to you, they try to have a conversation, and sometimes they start asking questions, but only to the point that you can answer. But what happens a lot is I tell them, "I don't know." I just don't understand it. I really want to study English, but until now, I haven't had time because we are working. If they are going to have us laid off for a long time I could study English.

Martha further explains how intercultural communication can pose a challenge to friendship and community organizing:

I have only lived in this city in the U.S. In Guatemala, when you go out to walk in the street, everyone greets you. We had a meeting with everyone here in town, but the people from here arrived and they didn't greet everyone. In Guatemala when you have a meeting you greet each person, and here they only say hello to the people they know. My husband felt sad because he really wanted to say hello to each of them. I don't really know people from the U.S., except for our priest. Some of our neighbors speak English, and they are friends of friends of ours, but I can't talk to them. It's the language barrier. Maybe they have the good intention of speaking to us, but you can only have contact with them if you speak English.

Martha is struggling to start an adult literacy program in the city, seeking out materials from Guatemala or Cuba, along with assistance from local schools. However, the women must have a Guatemalan ID card to enroll. She tires of governmental institutions assuming all people have driver's licenses, passports, and identification cards; they are completely out of touch with the poor, indigenous, and the undocumented. She fights for literacy because she sees communication as the abyss separating the women from their fellow community members, and also, with each new day, from their children who are trilingual and now speak more English than their parents. She describes their difficulties:

> The women don't organize together here, but in Guatemala, they do. Here they want to participate, but they don't know how, because of their limited English and their illiteracy in Spanish and in their Mayan languages. In Guatemala you can go to work and leave your children with your mom, and she takes care of them, and feeds them, but here, you don't know anyone, you don't have any relatives, there aren't people you can trust to take care of your children so you can study, and you need to work for income. It's a little difficult.

Literacy issues cross the border with the Mayan immigrants, a reality they try to conceal, and it is a nearly impossible situation. According to the World Bank Poverty Assessment, Guatemala's adult illiteracy level is 50 to 60 percent. In recent years access to primary education has become more universal, thus increasing literacy rates, shrinking the gender and economic gaps, and educating more indigenous. Males are still privileged when it comes to being educated, having literacy rates nearly 10 percent higher than females, but that spread has narrowed from 14 percent in 2000. The indigenous literacy gap overall has decreased by an impressive 9.1 percent from 2000 to 2006. According to Save the Children, 68 percent of indigenous women in Guatemala are illiterate. The Mayan women in Nebraska reflect this and lament that they were deprived of schooling during and after the civil war.

However, not all intelligence is acquired through formal education. Immigrants who negotiate the border acquire practical and experiential knowledge. Martha points out: "These are Indians. They can get anywhere, and do anything, and all on extremely limited resources. They are not used to living life with luxury." She is right. They are some of the most tested and capable people on earth.

José is working on his language skills as well: "I only speak a little bit of English. I am studying English at the library. Where I work they give us scholarships to study, and anyone who has an academic level that's a little high can receive one. I want to organize my time well, and study, because one of my goals is to become a teacher here."

The local adult ESL instructor is an energetic woman who exudes a love of life and is anxious to share her impressions about the effects the immigrants have had on her hometown. She teaches ESL, citizenship, and GED classes at an onsite learning center at a meatpacking plant. It's a partnership with a nearby community college that is funded by the plant, and they report attendance and test scores to the college. There is quarterly enrollment, with four orientations a year and courses lasting nine to twelve weeks. There are 160 students, some having logged over 400 hours of class time. A few years ago a new plant manager wanted to close the program to cut costs, but others convinced him how important it is to the community. The United Food and Commercial Workers (UFCW) union official noted they also contribute funds to keep the center in operation. The adult education classes are for anyone sixteen years and over and are open to the public, so 40 percent of the students are community members, rather than plant employees. The English classes are taught at different hours to cover all shifts. Students at the center are from Mexico, Honduras, El Salvador, Cuba, Guatemala, Sudan, Somalia, and Thailand, and there are as many as five different languages in the classroom at a time. The instructor beams, "It's the best job I've ever had. I love the students! They give me more than I give them." Her special affection for her students, both meatpacking employees and community members, is obvious: "For me, they're just like me and my family. They love their family, and they work hard for what's best for their kids. They work eight hours at the plant, and then take an English class for an hour and a half."

However, she says the immigrants' arrival has been a huge challenge for the city and the local school system. "We've become divided between those who question whether we are doing a good or poor job. Some people think immigrants are causing problems, but they are actually getting more by having them here. A few parents choose to not take their children to school here, so they are now driving them to other cities; some farmers don't want their kids going to school with 'Mexicans.' But now that is all better. It was worse before." Seeking out the positives, she exclaims, "We have the best avocados at the Mexican market, and the best *tacos de lengua*, tongue tacos, in the area! And it's all due to *the pack*! [Locals call the meatpacking plant the "pack".] Our city has changed. For the better!"

As our conversation draws to an end she shares that her dad worked at the plant for thirty-five years. She laughs, "It's a shock when he comes by the Learning Center and the students see a big, white guy who worked there and retired there! They can't believe it!" Reflecting, she states, "I am thankful to the *pack*. That's what my dad always called it, '*the pack*.' It was my family's livelihood. And I give thanks to all the people in the city of the pack! My kids will be better prepared to live in this world due to the cultural exposure they get here." Lastly, she informs me she will be selling their homegrown sweet corn tomorrow on a nearby corner. Her kids did that to help pay for university, and now that they are away, she continues marketing the bounty from their farm.

I recall Lucía telling me that when she arrived in Nebraska and saw all the cornfields, it reminded her of home, and she felt like staying. Again, corn, *la milpa*—the staple for making tortillas and the basic sustenance for life on earth—is an everyday yet very sacred ritualistic plant. Back home it was the most important thing in her life as it symbolized sustenance, and this is what she therefore honed in on upon arriving in Nebraska, a state largely made up of cornfields.

Nebraska is now among the top three states in corn production, and production is highest in the counties housing the meatpacking plants.[12] Lucía analyzes her new culture and the way corn is farmed here:

> It seems that what they do is better in the American culture, because they have machines. They have everything. However, in Guatemala, you have to go cultivate with your body, with your hands. You cut the corn with your hand, but here it's really different. From the first day I arrived here I saw that they were harvesting the corn, but with machines, with a tractor, and they sow the corn with a machine. In Guatemala you cut it, you pile the corn, *la milpa*, up, you shuck it, you start peeling it, so that all that's left is the ear, and you put it out to dry, and that's what you will use to make tortillas.

Some of the Guatemalan Mayan women left the agrarian life to seek out domestic or professional labor in their own country, and then continued on to do assembly-line work in Nebraska, on their quest for economic stability. They set out on their path to the unknown in the name of familial survival, but along the way they hope to grow, especially to learn to read and write and improve their English literacy. The Mayan women have become an integral part of the worker population in the meatpacking plants that are central to the communities and states housing them. Everyone living in their community has some type of relationship with the plants, and the next chapter will detail the central role meatpacking and the plants play in Nebraska cities and the Mayan women's lives.

5

Mayans and Meatpacking in Nebraska

After three years of curt refusals or outright disregard for our insistent requests, one plant finally agrees to give Martha and me a short tour. We are greeted and orientated about the dos and don'ts in the plant before we are led upstairs. I am a little nervous as I notice a few pieces of displaced red flesh while walking up the slippery stairs. There is an intense smell of raw meat and the floor is beyond slippery. Walking across the cafeteria floor is unsure; there is no way to get traction on it. Everyone is wearing safety helmets, protective glasses, and rubber boots, along with hairnets that cover their heads and beards. Bright orange earplugs hang around their necks. Some workers' white coats are relatively clean; others are splattered with blood both front and back. There is a quiet and seriousness in the plants; no one is overly friendly.

The supervisors are proud of their focus on worker comfort in this plant, which boasts lockers for each employee, a cafeteria that ensures every employee has a place to sit for lunch (rather than eating on the work floor or in the locker room), and a large parking lot for workers. Employees have left their lunchboxes at their clean, chosen spot in the cafeteria, and some are there, watching television while silently eating their lunches or sharing things on their cellphones with fellow employees. They don't notice us much at all. We are just more visitors. There is a general quiet and calm.

We are then led through a stainless-steel maze. Right before we go around the last corner to walk through the door to enter the cutting floor we are told to put in our earplugs. I don't want to, because I want to hear the noise level, but I comply. Once inside

I am glad to have the noise level muffled as it makes the whole experience rather surrealistic. Suddenly we are in this roiling sea of blood-red beef. There is meat everywhere. It is coming around on hooks, traveling across conveyor belts, sliding down chutes, disappearing through other slots, swinging around on pulleys, dropping through holes in the belt and out onto other belts, and everything is in motion, all at once, and it never stops. It is hard to focus on any one place. The air is quite cool and damp. It smells like meat and cold beef fat. We take constant care, having been warned not to slip and fall.

Sometimes we slide through tiny areas where someone is in a corner at a sink washing utensils or doing some other task, and they hug the wall or sink to let us by. Everyone has a designated spot and job to do, and we are the awkward intruders. No one is off task. Everyone is focused and has some kind of utensil or two in their bloodstained, gloved hands. They all appear to be wearing many layers under their white coats, having a somewhat padded physique. They stand on bloodstained, cushioned floor mats, hugging the line and performing their specific task on every piece of meat that comes their way, often piling them up in their work area when too many come at once, then diligently working through them and sending them on their way. The noise level does not permit conversation; the entire tour consists of maybe ten words shouted by the guide directly into my left ear. At the beginning he states the beef carcass is divided in two and signals the two different directions in which the half carcasses then travel. These half pieces swing around, and workers standing in a line made up almost entirely of men each take a knife and saw down the entire length, cutting out huge pieces of it. Those pieces head down belts weaving all over the place. It is too hard to follow all the beef in motion and identify where it is going. As we walk through one tight space, some pieces of beef as large as my torso swing on an overhead conveyor and drip water on us. I am scared, wondering what would happen if one fell off the hook onto our heads. As we walk under a chute I notice cut-off pieces of fat falling through a slot, and I see workers' legs on the other side of it.

We are then escorted up onto a catwalk. The stairs are made of stainless-steel grid and are also coated in grease—or beef fat, to be more specific. We have been told to hold onto both railings, and although they are greasy I clench them tightly. Now upstairs, perched above the workers, we observe them processing all the beef. I admire all the simultaneous work going on below. This is a highly ordered, nonstop procedure. Everyone is doing one job, but doing it constantly and continuously. The employees who cut the largest pieces arriving on hooks against the far wall have a sharpener and knife; after each cut they poise their sharpeners on their shoulders to sharpen their knives in a violin-playing position. They also seem to move about in place on the line as one worker sometimes takes longer than the others to execute his or her long cut on the moving carcass. I admire the way they move their bodies into or away from the piece half their own size to get better momentum for the tremendous cut they are making. The pieces they cut off then head to another area where they are further cut down, and the remaining piece heads in another direction. Some workers have a shaver apparatus and shave all the fat off the meat. Others remove an oval-shaped bone, over and over. Some use a knife to remove the fat from large pieces with ribs. Another group is using electric knives to cut the meat off the bones. No one moves from his or her place, and everyone is focused on the work. The faces of the workers in the plant are Mexican, Mayan, Cuban, Somali . . . mostly multiethnic, but also Anglo. In the cafeteria and walking through the hallways many languages are heard. The workers are mostly young, in their twenties and thirties, but there are people of all ages. We silently observe them working. Some make eye contact with us, seemingly wondering who we are, or keeping an eye on the supervisor who accompanies us. We have been told not to speak to any workers, so we don't. If we do, the tour is over. It's a tremendous safety breach.

As we turn to leave, a worker who had moved rapidly down the catwalk stairs moments before, carrying a piece of meat I wouldn't have been able to lift, is now coming back up the stairs as quickly as he can. I am afraid for his life as those stairs are so greasy, but he easily makes it up and past us before we head down. They are used to maneuvering on this slippery floor. We are taken around more corners through the meat maze and peek into the other side where a similar scene is in full action; this is the other half of the carcass going in the other direction. I try to imagine being a worker in the plant. I am glad that I have my earplugs and that they have theirs. It is the swimming pool effect; they are in the plant, closely surrounded by many others, but the earplugs close them off into their own little world of lapping through the many cuts that will make up their eight-hour work shift.

We are then taken to an area where they prepare the meat for export to Japan and Mexico. We are told 80 percent of the meat is for export, and 15 percent goes to Walmart and McDonald's. This area is quiet, nearly silent, because the meat is already vacuum packed, and the workers are simply labeling it. It's also more dimly lit, and thus, more relaxing. One woman checks skirt steaks one by one, holding them up and flipping them over, then piling them up for packaging. Next to her is a bin overflowing with all the cartilage that she has removed from them. I spot what appear to be cow tongues in packages as well, and later we are told these are skinned and exported to Japan, and priced at a rate much higher than in the United States. We cross an open area to a walk-in freezer door. I can tell this is going to be a "ta-dah" moment by the look on the guide's face. The door is swung open and inside reveals endless curlicue rows of entire beef carcasses swinging around on hooks on a steel belt hanging from the ceiling. They curve to and fro in a silent death waltz, weaving their way back and forth, to eventually end up on the cut floor we have just left. I have never seen so many tons of raw meat in my life. I am in awe. Who eats all this meat? I'm also afraid, trying to stay out of the way and close to the wall, and wondering how hard you would fall if one of those massive blood red carcasses hit you from behind while you weren't looking. We are proudly told the plant processes 375 animals a day.

Everyone we spoke to inside the plant, both supervisors and union representatives, had also worked on the floor, for years. For them it is the most natural thing on earth, to work at a meat-packing plant. It's a job born out of their physical location in the United States, on the Nebraska plains. They say it's hard the first few days, but then your body builds up resistance and you get stronger, and it isn't much effort. However, I note they all now hold supervisory jobs, having been promoted, and do not work on the floor any longer. Some of the union representatives are elected by the workers, but if their term ends and they are not reelected, they go back to the line. They say that working at the plant pays more than minimum wage, and some who work over-time raise their earnings substantially. The quiet on the line, the focused work ethic, the seriousness and the calm about the work made me realize that for them it really is just their job. It's what they do to earn their wage and pay their bills. They are working, in the Midwest, in the jobs that are available.

The Mayan women have landed in just the right place to ben-efit from the work available in Nebraska's meatpacking plants. All the interviewees either worked at a plant or had a spouse who supported the family by working there. The plants are the puls-ing heart of both the community and local economy. Everyone, from the workers to union officials, bank directors, law officials, and social service providers are well aware of their interrelated-ness with the plants. The immigrants came to work in the plants, but how did the plants end up in rural Nebraska cities?

Beef cattle are Nebraska's single largest industry and the force powering the economy. The story of beef is the story of a migra-tion from south to north, as cattle came to North America with the Spanish in the late 1400s. The large herds that roamed the Texas plains were derived from the Spanish cattle, and many of those cowboys, or *vaqueros*, who pushed cattle into Nebraska in the 1870s were Mexican. Between 1900 and 1929, sizeable numbers of Mexicans came to Nebraska, pushed by political and economic crises in their home country and pulled by jobs in the beet fields of western Nebraska as well as the stockyards and packing houses, principally in South Omaha.[1]

The Mexicans have herded cattle up into the northern terrain since the Spaniards arrived in the Americas, and their native language provided the terms used today in cowboy and rodeo culture: lasso, rodeo, bronco, chaps, pinto, and lariat are all derived from Spanish. English-speaking cowboys mispronounced the Spanish words, thus creating Spanglish terms for their cowboy gear, cattle, and horses. Recall, prior to 1848, that Mexico included the territories of California, Nevada, Utah, Arizona, New Mexico, and Texas, as well as parts of Wyoming, Colorado, Oklahoma, and Kansas, but with the signing of the Treaty of Guadalupe Hidalgo in 1848, the United States received more than half of Mexico's territory. Throughout history, the arrival of the Spaniards has influenced the Mayans' lives and culture, with people, crops, and animals moving freely across man-made borders before they even existed.

Meatpacking arrived with the cattle in the 1880s, especially in Iowa and Nebraska. In the early days the plants were built in major cities such as Omaha and Kansas City, close to train transportation and the plentiful labor force, but since the mid-1900s the plants have relocated to rural areas to be closer to the animals along with the railroad and highways. In rural areas there is more space for cattle feedlots, and the animals can be raised, slaughtered, and packaged within a smaller area. Originally slaughterhouses shipped carcasses to retail meat markets for cutting and packaging, but slowly smaller box-packing plants that slaughtered and cut up sides of beef were developed, and retailers reduced most of their "butchering employees."

The stockyards and packing plants have attracted immigrant laborers for decades. African Americans from the middle southern states started arriving in the early 1900s, helping to double the Nebraska population in ten years, and this influx led to social, economic, and racial conflicts.[2] When the plants later moved to rural areas, Spanish-speaking people and other ethnic groups arrived in large numbers to fill the jobs. History repeats itself as the transnational migrations triggered by changing economies supply laborers for the meatpacking plants.[3] Immigration is tightly interwoven with the corn, cattle, and meatpacking industries in Nebraska, as well as in the global economy.

After World War II, diesel technology, antibiotics, fertilizers, and herbicides boosted corn production, leading to expanded cattle-feeding operations. Extensive, fuel-powered transportation systems also encouraged higher production. Feedlots proliferated as a result. According to Nebraska Beef Council, the state has the top three beef-production counties in the nation, and cattle outnumbered Nebraskans nearly four to one in 2012. Nebraska's $6.6 billion in agricultural exports in 2013 translate into $8.1 billion in additional economic activity; altogether, the state's beef production makes a $12.1 billion impact on Nebraska's economy. In addition, Nebraska ranks first in the United States for commercial red meat production and slaughter.[4] Meat is Nebraska's largest export, generating $5.1 billion in 2012.[5] As world trade grows, Nebraska plays a role in the global economy while the meatpacking plants and all related work remain critical to the local economies that house them.

Employment in the Plants

After meatpacking shifted to rural areas, shortages in the local labor force developed. Employees in these unionized meatpacking plants used to earn more than many factory workers, but wages have steadily decreased, becoming so low that companies began recruiting among the immigrant workforce, both locally and globally. The U.S. Department of Labor reports there were 75,620 domestic and foreign slaughter and meatpacking employees who earned an annual mean wage of $24,940 in 2012, with hourly wages ranging from $8.76 to $15.71. There is a steady flow of immigrant laborers from poverty-stricken populations abroad appearing to fill the low-paid assembly-line jobs that don't require English skills or much job training, and that pay a much higher hourly wage than at home. However, due to the low wages and the strenuous and repetitive nature of the work, the plants have a high employee turnover rate.

Small cities in Nebraska—among them, Lexington, Grand Island, South Sioux City, Schuyler, and Fremont—house some of the meatpacking plants that attract immigrants such as the Mayans who are looking for work to fund their *remesas*, remittances or money wires, back to Guatemala. Early on meatpacking employees were largely from central and eastern Europe; today, many of Nebraska's food processing workers come from Latin America, Africa, and Southeast Asia. One large plant advertised on radio stations that could be heard in Mexico, and companies have been known to pay recruits' bus fares to the United States, putting them up in local hotels and lending them money for food and work clothes until they get settled in. Cuban, Thai, and Somali workers from Miami arrived as well. There is a trailer court right next to one plant; the sheriff noted that it has been taken over by the Sudanese working in the plant, adding, "The pack has had to change, and get interpreters in there, to deal with the issues all the immigrant workers bring." Some of the workers move to the meatpacking cities, others rent a room in town, and some live in nearby urban cities and commute to the plants, taking the second shift from 2:00 p.m. to 10:30 p.m.

Often supervisors who attracted workers received bonuses. Nowadays, kinship ties usually draw immigrants to where they will have family, friends, and work. The Mayans interviewed here all knew someone when they arrived.

The UFCW is a union that boasts 1.3 million members nationwide, 250,000 of which are in meatpacking and food processing. The union proclaims the interconnectedness of farmers, ranchers, workers, and rural communities. The local UFCW official states that in one plant with 1,800 employees there are 1,300 workers in production, and 95 percent of the employees are Hispanic, including Mexican, Guatemalan, Salvadoran, Cuban, Peruvian, Nicaraguan, and Venezuelan. There are also employees from Vietnam, Ethiopia, a few from India, and 200 Burmese, Somalis, and Sudanese. Thirteen languages are spoken in the plant.

The Mayan women are quite guarded about their work at the plant, stating it is just a job. However, each relates a bit about their experience working in the plants. According to Manuela:

> I started working at this meatpacking plant not long ago. I was working at another packing plant in a different town, but I had to commute an hour each way, leaving at 5:00 a.m. and coming back at 5:00 p.m., and I have a daughter, so I quit. She is almost three years old, and I have a son back home, with my dad, but we are going to bring him here because here you are better off. In Guatemala there's work, but it's very low paid, and things are really expensive there. Here, when you work all week, you have money, and as much food as you want.

Both Juana and her husband work there too: "Here I work at the plant. I have my two children and my husband and we both work the night shift, from 2:45 p.m. to 11:15 p.m. at the plant. Thank God we are both working. When I am working, the children go to a woman who takes care of them. I only work from Monday to Friday, and they pay me on time. It seems like a good job to me." Lucía is pleased to have work as well: "Now I work six days a week, forty to forty-eight hours, and they pay us more if we work overtime, but you just take the hours available. Some of the workers come out smiling with their check because they worked extra, and when they look at their check they get really happy."

María was hired at the plant despite her lack of valid papers, something that would be nearly impossible today, due to E-Verify, an electronic program that the Illegal Immigration Reform and Immigrant Responsibility Act of 1996, IIRIRA, requires employers to use. It is a computer-based employment verification program that matches Social Security numbers and names in order to screen potential employees and verify their legal status to work, thus preventing the hiring of undocumented workers. María tells how she acquired employment with papers she purchased:

> At the plant I have a different name; the boss and everyone call me Maricruz, but that's not the way it is, it's a little trick I played. I don't have papers, so I work with someone else's. Sometimes, I get to thinking, in God's eyes, is what I'm doing correct? I hope God can pardon me for what necessity can lead one to do. I've gotten used to the name Maricruz, because I have been using it for years. When I was new, and somebody asked my name, I would stay silent for a long while and tell them, "Sometimes they call me Maricruz," but I knew it wasn't my name, and I would feel bad, but little by little, I got used to it.
>
> I give thanks to God, for the papers, and that everything came out okay, because I bought different ones in the beginning, and when I went to the interview they asked me if the papers were really mine, because the person on those papers was in jail for a long time. "You are a thief!" they told me, and I got scared. "Nooooooo," I told him, "I am going to take care of my papers," and they didn't say anything else to me. I tore up those papers, with fear, because they could call the police, and put me in jail, and besides that, if they report it, they could deport me. But no, they don't want that at the meatpacking plant, thank God, they don't want that.

The plants are most interested in finding employees who have valid permission to work. Acquiring the proper paperwork for employment is costly, but quite possible in the United States. Some of the undocumented workers even rent their papers to others on a weekly basis when they are not using them, a practice they call "putting the papers to work."

As to documentation status in the plants, the UFCW official states:

> A lot of the employees are undocumented, but the plants pretend they don't know that, and we, the union, have a "don't ask, don't

tell" policy. Since 2012 they use E-Verify, but before that about 50 percent were undocumented. About five years ago, with E-Verify, they terminated three hundred people in one week, and some of them had been working in the plant for ten years. In our office we see one or two document falsifications per week, but it is usually people who have been in the plant for more than ten years so the notification must be coming down from ICE.

The question remains regarding how many of the workers in the plants are undocumented. ICE has required the plants to use the federal E-Verify program. In February 2012 the U.S. House of Representatives Judiciary Committee approved E-Verify (on a thirteen to eight vote), and in September 2012 the House of Representatives passed a bill reauthorizing the program for three more years. ICE has steadily increased the number of deportations in the past ten years, and this may be affecting the number of undocumented immigrant laborers and their decisions to either stay or return home.[6]

At the UFCW office the official orientates an endless line of meatpacking plant employees. She helps them with such predicaments as hiring, training, salary, and interpreting, and she assists with direct deposit or use of bank accounts. She outlines her role:

> The union gets a list of new hires, with each employee's job and department, and then there are two days of orientation for them, but all the rules and information are too much in just two days so the employees forget. There are rules for missing work, being late, or calling in sick, and it is all on a point system.
>
> Language is also an issue. The people from Africa and Burma don't speak English, and those from Guatemala don't speak English or Spanish so we bring an interpreter to the orientation, and now the company has interpreters on the floor. There are union stewards supporting in the plant and they speak Spanish. They are union members, but they have language limitations, so we also help them make appointments with doctors or counselors. One woman's husband is in jail and there is no interpreter for

her because she speaks a Mayan language. The employees at the union offices in three other cities do not speak any Spanish, so we interpret for their employees as well.

The employees send their workmates to us for help. The Muslims need to pray during the work day, so the plant tries to work with them, but it's hard on production, which is just profit oriented. Another woman has a little boy with disabilities. It's very difficult. They also need help with immigration forms! They need to fill out applications online for U.S. citizenship or residency, and we help them because the income tax places and notaries charge so much to fill out applications. All the information they need is on the resident card, so I learned the process, and now I can fill out residency forms in about an hour, and citizenship in two hours, doing it all online at the USCIS website.

Sometimes there are conflicts between employees and supervisors and then we get involved, and report it to HR. Sometimes people do get fired. Most of the worker complaints are about fast work and injuries, or giving women men's jobs, or there may be an error in their payment since different jobs have different hourly wages, and if their supervisor switches their post but forgets to note it down on their time card, the payment is incorrect, so we report it to HR and they pay it out. If there were a conflict at that point, we would report it to the Department of Labor.

There are different departments such as knives, packing, boxing. After six months employees can bid to change jobs, even for supervisor. The union controls bids; the employees fill out the forms and the company decides who can move. There is a large turnover at the plant; twenty new hires a week, and ten to twenty leave each week. Reasons for termination range from breaking safety laws, or absence due to illness or family problems, or for fighting or stealing.

She patiently reminds all the workers of plant rules and fields nonstop phone calls throughout our conversation, reminding them that they must call thirty minutes in advance if they are sick and that they will need a doctor's note if they are off work for more than three days.

A community member's husband has been working at the plant for eleven years. In the past there were three shifts, but when his job, load out, was taken over by robots, the number of people needed in that position dropped from forty to seven. At the plant, shifts and benefits are awarded based on seniority, so her husband didn't get let go. He started out working on the floor, but after three years he was under so much stress that he got sick. He would come home so tired he would sleep from the moment he got home from work until he had to go back. So he quit and went to work in a nearby dairy for a year. Because of a new boss and an imposed shift change at the dairy, he returned to the plant and took the night shift, knowing that after six months workers can bid for different jobs and move to a different department. Other community members interviewed had worked at the plants as well, but not for long. One man lasted only thirty days due to the duress, but his brother stayed on longer than that. Another woman worked in both beef- and pork-packing plants, but quit and changed careers once she became pregnant at the age of eighteen. She recalls the work was always done in a hurry.

The UFCW official points out that the plants donate money to local schools and community buildings and projects and promote free English and citizenship classes at the job site or in local community centers. UFCW helps with the paperwork, and one plant had thirty-five new citizens in the year that we spoke. The union shares the employees' joy when they realize that their children will automatically become citizens. The union provides immigration clinics as each new policy change goes into action, largely to undercut the disreputable businesses offering overpriced services to immigrants. The plants also contribute to scholarships for local high school graduates and offer them a chance to work for the summer at the plant, either to try it on as a career or to earn money while on break from university. She ponders, "To a certain degree the people running the plant care, but they care more about getting the work done, especially if they are in the middle of a big job."

One plant stated that establishing a better relationship between the plants and the community has been one of their most important goals for the past few years. They sponsor the Hispanic Festival, county fairs, and other events in town. They meet with community leaders to identify issues the plants can target, and when the need for more prekindergarten education was identified, they supported school bonds that will make it possible to build a new elementary school in one city. They boast that community members now know they can come to them about civic concerns; they donate meat for raffles to support community projects, or they donate money or match funds raised by the workers for community causes like supporting ailing fellow employees or paying for burials. The UFCW negotiated a benefit of a multicultural fund, and now the schools or city entities can go directly to the human resources department to receive funds for multicultural events. One plant donates meat so that veterans can raise money to travel to the war memorials in Washington, D.C., a much-appreciated gesture acknowledged in the local newspaper. They also do service projects to help the community: when one city suffered two major floods, the plant asked workers if they wanted the plant to halt production so that workers could do relief work, and the workers opted to clean up after the flood, using equipment provided by the plant.

In the community, everyone interviewed had an understanding of the reciprocal need the plants and the workers have for one another; no one seemed to feel aggression or animosity toward the other. The UFCW official assured, "We are all connected in these packing towns, and we have a close plant/worker relationship that is not often betrayed. If anyone is hesitant to talk to you it is because they are concerned about their paperwork or lack thereof." The plants are not focused on enforcing immigration laws; they need documented, able-bodied employees.

Anti-Immigrant Sentiments in the
Receiving Communities

At times, however, tensions over labor and legal rights quickly bubble to the surface. Juana states that some of the people in the city where she lives do not like the Latinos who have arrived, and there has been legislation that reflects her assessment.[7] Nebraska Appleseed Center for Law in the Public Interest states that anti-immigrant sentiment in Nebraska is caused by misguided and harmful public policy designed to create fear and division among neighbors. However, for the most part, the Mayans don't complain about their jobs or the way they are treated in their cities or at the plants, probably because they don't want to draw any attention to the plants and their livelihood—especially not negative attention, in the fear that they might lose their jobs as many did during the ICE raids. Operation Wagon Train, the largest enforcement in U.S. history, took place in Swift meatpacking plants in six different states in December 2006. Others were deported in December 2000 when the Immigration and Naturalization Service, INS, raided Nebraska Beef in Omaha, and in 1999 as well, when Operation Vanguard conducted verifications at Nebraska meatpacking plants to identify workers who lacked proper work authorization. Many church, business, and union leaders pulled together to voice opposition, arguing that these raids are racist, anti-immigrant, and disruptive to communities, meatpacking plants, and Nebraska's economy. INS replaced occasional raids with comprehensive investigations of employment eligibility records in an effort to locate undocumented workers.[8] In this way, the INS is targeting what draws immigrants to Nebraska, estimating that as much as 25 percent of the meatpacking workforce is undocumented immigrants. Many such people left before the investigation began, fearing the trauma of being singled out and unwanted once again.

Martha sadly narrated that during the ICE raids many Mayans fled to the cornfields to hide in fear, just as they had done when their communities were burned and massacred in Guatemala. The

ICE raids in the meatpacking plants have devastating effects on Mayan immigrants in rural Nebraska, creating panic and massive fleeing, a Mayan exodus that recalls the genocidal civil war for them. Feeling marginalized and targeted for violence and persecution is not new for Mayans. Again, U.S. immigration policy needs to address the issues raised by undocumented workers. Human rights organizations voice concern over the lingering psychosocial effects the raids have had on the workers.[9]

After the ICE *redadas*, raids, the investigations, and the new E-Verify system, conditions returned to near normal in the rural communities. Two of the undocumented people interviewed can no longer work at the plants, but they still work in rural Nebraska. The plants have attracted lots of Thai and other immigrants with valid work papers. Their legal status allows them to approach the job with a less strenuous work ethic; they just don't *need* to work as much as the undocumented do. Again, the meatpacking plant and the workers are constantly changing to follow current policy and practices.

Meatpacking Worker Rights, Income, and Remittances

Human rights organizations research worker rights in the plants, but none of the women complained about sexual or physical abuse. However, the sister of a young, Anglo Nebraskan woman who took a job at a plant only lasted three months because of the sexual harassment she experienced. Women other than the Mayans reported that there was much promiscuity in the workplace and that supervisors have been known to use their rank in a competitive fashion among themselves to secure sexual trysts with the employees working under them. However, the UFCW official said conflicts are infrequent because the plant is proactive and deals with situations before they escalate to the level that would necessitate union and HR involvement.

Although the Mayans did not complain about their treatment, one of the women did report a problem with a supervisor at the plant:

In the beginning, when I first started, I felt that the supervisor wasn't treating me well. He is a really mean supervisor, always on your back. He's Mexican so he speaks Spanish. And he's always watching over you, saying, "You have to do it this way," but since you are new, you don't know how the work is done. So one day I just got mad, because he was always scolding me, and I told him to go look carefully at the pieces and check whose they were. He realized it was another worker sending the pieces out wrong, and asked me to pardon him. And I told him it was unfair of him to scold me, and shout at me. We pay dues that come out of each paycheck, and there's a union that defends us if they treat us badly, so I warned him, "If you keep treating me like this, I am going to go to the union." He knows, if someone goes to complain to the union, he will be reprimanded, and that will affect how they evaluate him as a supervisor. Sometimes they even suspend them. So I warned him before I went to complain to the union. And from then on he didn't do it anymore, and now he doesn't say anything to me. Now he treats me well. You start feeling hopeless when they mistreat you, and besides that, the Americans check over our work as well, and you can't talk to them in English, but you can talk with the supervisor, and you can complain.

With support from the union, her conflict was resolved. The women quickly learn what their rights are, as protected by labor unions or state laws, and they are willing to use these organizations for protection.

OSHA oversees workplace safety in the United States, including in the meatpacking plants. According to the UFCW official, "Safety in the plants is a big issue because it's wet, and there's meat and bone on the floor. Therefore, there's no running, and they always need to wear their ear plugs. The plant reviews the OSHA regulations at orientation." One worker did speak to me about the seriousness of working in the plant; the knives are very sharp, and the line is always moving, so the workers need to be calm and pay close attention to the work at hand to avoid accidents. Ensuring that everyone is safe is very important to the Mayan workers, and they also make sure the supervisor has someone substitute for them when they need to use the restroom or are physically tired of doing a certain job.[10] This is a working community like any other.

Nebraska produces one of every five steaks and hamburgers in the country, and meatpacking workers collectively can make up to 20,000 cuts per day in order to prepare the meat for consumers. These numerous repetitive motions often lead to ergonomic injuries,[11] and often the injury is not noticed until the effects have become crippling. In one local newspaper, a massage therapist advertised in Spanish for services for sore muscles and injuries, knowing the local population and the types of corporal problems that working in the meatpacking plants may produce. Some human rights groups suspect that plants discourage reporting work-related injuries to keep their safety infractions record low. They also fear employers may threaten to report immigration status, and this keeps employees from reporting injuries or illnesses. There is a lot of criticism against the meatpacking plants.[12]

However, the Mayans interviewed complained very little about the plants or their employers. When I pressed for more information, they told me that they don't want to speak negatively about the plants, nor do they want me to do that. It is just a job. They work and support their families both here and abroad, and they are thankful the plants pay them on time. One employee tells me they are tired of people coming in to the plants under false pretenses and then publishing videos and photographs they were not authorized to take. The ESL instructor at one of the plants says, "Some of the jobs are really hard, and others are easy but boring. Clean-up is the most difficult job ever. When I ask the Latinos how they feel about their jobs they say, 'Yes! I like my job,' but later, after we get to know each other better and there is more trust, they say, 'I *hate* my job.'"

In 2001, the state of Nebraska adopted the Nebraska Meatpacking Industry Workers Bill of Rights, a law that improved meatpacking health and safety conditions. It includes the right to organize, to a safe workplace, to adequate facilities and the opportunity to utilize them, to adequate equipment, to complete and understandable information, to existing state and federal benefits and rights, to freedom from discrimination, and to continued training, including supervisor training. And in 2003 the Non–English-Speaking Workers Protection Act was passed in Nebraska to assist non–English-speaking workers with understanding the terms and conditions of their employment. It requires employers who seek such workers to provide interpreters and written statements in the workers' native languages regarding their hours, wages, and responsibilities. It codified the Nebraska law and created a part-time position for a Nebraska meatpacking workers' rights coordinator.[13]

Human rights organizations such as Nebraska Appleseed and Human Rights Watch have done extensive studies of employee abuses in the meatpacking plants and urge immigrants to stand up for worker rights, regardless of their status. They believe that a humane and workable immigration system should become a national priority. In 2010, OSHA reviewed the Appleseed survey findings and took the recommendations into consideration. Human Rights Watch also warns against violating worker rights: "U.S. immigration and labor law and policy fail to respect and ensure the rights guaranteed to all non-citizen workers, irrespective of their immigration status, by international human rights law."[14] The Mayans working in the meatpacking plants did not address these abuse concerns. However, the hardships some of the Mayan immigrants have suffered may make them simply more resilient to physical labor demands.

The Mayan women are concerned about the physical duress of the job and how long their thirty-something female bodies will be able to sustain it. Juana voices her worry: "Sometimes I start thinking this job is really physically hard on me, it's not so easy. When I started, I was working Saturdays too. It's strenuous, but thank God I have a job, and when I have seniority they will give me another job."

Lucía feels the job is wearing on her body as well:

Now I've been working in a beef plant an hour away for two years. I know that all jobs in that plant are tiring, but it is going well for me, thank God. It was harder in the other plant where I worked for a year. I got pregnant while I was working there, and since I didn't have proper papers to be working, and they realized I was already eight months along, they changed my job position, and sent me to clean the office. I already had a huge belly, so I mopped, swept, and took out the trash in the supervisor's office. He was a really good person.

In this case the humanity of the supervisor shines through when she was not let go once it was discovered she was pregnant, but rather given more gentle work. The reciprocal care attitude resurfaces. But Lucía still wonders how long her body will sustain the work:

Now, thank God, my family in Guatemala has something to eat, even if it's just the customary beans, tortilla, and tamales. One day I want to go back to Guatemala, but I don't want to stay there because it's so difficult there. The day is going to come when I just can't work anymore so I will have to leave this country. Sometimes, in the plant you realize you are already too old to work in that company. You can't do it anymore. And sometimes the people can't go on. You are already tired out, your body is too, and you already feel that the work is too hard.

The women need the income from the job, but they also realize it won't be physically viable for them forever.

María expresses the joy it brings her to be able to work and assist her family financially:

Just yesterday I spoke with my dad and my mom. I know I am helping them, and they feel happy. I am giving them everything

I can, and I also have to pay for food, rent, and those kinds of things here. I don't have a set amount that I send to them, but now I am going to send them $300 with a man who is going to Guatemala and he will go by and give them the money. At Christmas, or in December, I sent them $1,000. That way they have money, in case they need to buy things to spend time with the family. I sent $1,000, but I also bought clothes, shoes, and blankets. I send it all a box that we buy here, and the post office charges us $165 to send it, but you can put whatever you want in it. I buy it all new. For example, my mom didn't have a blender, so I sent her one, and that way they can make themselves juice. I buy the things one by one here, I gather them up little by little, and when it's all full I send it to them, but it is always a lot of money. When the neighbors receive a box my parents get really sad, so I want to send one to my parents too.

María explains how her salary at the plant fluctuates, based on the workload available, thus impacting the amount she can send home to her family in Guatemala: "My salary varies. I used to make $1,500 a check, but recently they cut our hours and I am now earning $1,300. I hope the situation with the meat improves soon. I save a lot so I can send as much as possible to Guatemala." As María details, the work at the plant isn't always stable, as outbreaks of E. coli, mad cow disease, or "pink slime" affect consumer demands. The workers fear anything that stops production and therefore the need for their labor.

Juana expresses her concern as well: "Sometimes we work forty hours, but this week it was only thirty-six hours, because the workload has gone down. No one has been laid off yet, the people are working, but they haven't said what's going to happen after this." Any issues affecting meat production decrease immigrant workloads.

In December of 2003, a dairy cow in Washington State was found to have bovine spongiform encephalopathy, BSE, more commonly known as mad cow disease. The U.S. Department of

Agriculture, USDA, immediately conducted a study and advised American consumers they were not in danger and that a single case was no threat to public health. However, the effects on international trade were devastating; just one cow infected with the disease set off a wave of fear among global consumers. When Escherichia coli (E. coli), a form of food poisoning, occurs, or when the use of "pink slime"—ammonia-treated beef filler added to hamburger—is brought to the public's attention, consumers become frightened and popular national foodstuffs such as hamburger are suddenly scrutinized, lowering consumption and therefore production demands. Situations like this impact the state's beef economy, and in turn both local and international economies. Outbreaks of E. coli, mad cow disease, and "pink slime" send workers into another type of panic. The people working in the plants are laid off, or *descansados*, rested, as Juana and Lucía say, when the demand for meat goes down. If laid off, more adverse poverty ensues, and workers are forced to rely on local social services to supply food and health assistance.

Accustomed to working forty to forty-eight hours a week, Lucía was laid off at the time of her interview:

> Now, in the company where I work, they laid all of us off for three to five weeks. This, for us, is really bad. They say they are going to pay us, but I don't know yet. We'll receive our last check this week, and then wait to see if they are going to pay us again. They're not selling anything because they say no cows are coming out of Canada right now, and that's where the cows come from. I'm thinking it's that mad cow disease, or others say they want to raise the price, because the cows are expensive. And once the price of cattle goes up a bit, they will start more production, and they will hire us back.

For the workers, lacking the income much needed to support their local and international families has global consequences. It exacerbates the poverty they are trying to overcome through transnational migrations to seek work at the plants.

The Banco de Guatemala, the Bank of Guatemala, shows that from 2008 to 2011 approximately $40 billion were sent annually from the United States in *remesas,* remittances. This has become the backbone of the economy, and the departments with the most emigrants gain the most economic support from abroad. This takes the pressure off the regional governments' social service spending. The IOM restates remittance amounts: Almost all (97.6 percent) are sent from the United States, and each household received, on average, about US$306 per month. Guatemala's remittances now exceed the total volume of its annual exports or income from tourism and are now a pillar of the Guatemalan economy, benefiting more than 1.5 million people.[15]

Earlier the *remesas* typically went for necessities such as food and shelter, but as María notes, now they are used for extra household items and appliances. According to Smith, "Those who emigrate are normally between 20 and 45 years old. . . . Almost 22 percent of remittance recipients are heads of household, of whom 23.3 percent are indigenous and 76.7 percent nonindigenous. Others benefiting are spouses (11.8 percent), children (48.7 percent), grandchildren (10 percent), parents and parents-in-law (1.5 percent), brothers and sisters (1.4 percent), and other relatives."[16] However, according to this study, the *remesas* are not reducing overall poverty levels at the rate that would be expected.

To facilitate these transfers, local money-wiring offices have opened in the meatpacking cities, but the Mayans have experienced problems with some of the courier companies. For example, one company turned the names of immigrants using their services over to ICE. The immigrants responded with a boycott, which continues today.

Latino Migrants Transform Nebraska Communities

The Latino population in the United States grew more than 40 percent over the last decade. Hispanics accounted for over half of the nation's growth and have become the largest minority in the country. According to Passel et al. the 2010 census showed Hispanics numbered 50.5 million and made up 16 percent of the U.S. population. In Nebraska, from 1990 to 2000, the increase was the tenth highest in the nation at 155 percent. One study of unauthorized immigrants estimates there are about 11 million here, but the Pew Hispanic Center reports immigration through Mexico has nearly come to a standstill due to the weakened U.S. job market, heightened border enforcement, a rise in deportations, the growing dangers associated with illegal border crossings, and changing economic and demographic conditions in Mexico. This same study states that unauthorized immigrants make up 3.7 percent of the nation's population and 5.2 percent of its labor force; 58 percent of these unauthorized immigrants are Mexican.

Many immigrating Latinos have chosen to come to Nebraska, and most are living in rural cities. Lexington, located in south-central Nebraska, has been called "Mexington" to reflect its changing demographics, and it is in one of the fastest growing counties with a population of 10,230 in 2010 according to governmental data.[17] It is the home of Tyson Fresh Foods, a nonunionized plant with 2,450 employees that opened in 1990. Lexington began in 1860 as an early frontier trading post near the Platte River on the Oregon Trail, a trail traversed by more than half a million Americans before the Union Pacific Railroad was completed. In the 1870s, railroad workers and homesteaders who came to farm the free land moved into the area. Many large ranches sprang up along the Platte River, and thousands of cattle roamed the free range. Nowadays, the economy in Lexington revolves around manufacturing, retailing, meat processing, aquaculture, alfalfa dehydrating, cattle feeding, farming, ranching, and ethanol production. East of Lexington, in central Nebraska, Grand Island had a population of 48,520 in the 2010 census. The unionized JBS Swift meatpacking plant was established there in 1979, and it employs 3,300, making it the city's largest employer.

Northeast, in Columbus, Cargill employs four hundred non-unionized employees. In 1968 Excel, a subsidiary of Cargill Meat Solutions, opened a plant in Schuyler, a small east-central city

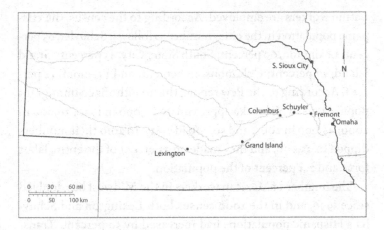

2. Map of Nebraska, courtesy Bill Nelson.

with a population of 6,269. The plant now has two thousand employees—twice as many men as women—and is unionized with UFCW as well. The town was founded in 1887 and settled by mostly European immigrants, but nowadays there is a near-Hispanic majority. In 2010, 28 percent of the population in Schuyler was bilingual, and 48 percent of the bilingual inhabitants spoke Spanish. From 1990 to 1995, the number of Hispanics employed at the Cargill plant tripled, and in 2004 Hispanics held 85 percent of the jobs. Fremont, also in eastern Nebraska, has 26,397 inhabitants. Fremont Beef Company employs three hundred, and unionized Hormel Foods Corporation employs 1,425.

In the northeast corner of the state, South Sioux City's population was 13,353 in 2010. It is growing twice as fast as other towns in Nebraska, with a 23 percent rate of growth since 1990. About 25 percent of its inhabitants are fluent in Spanish, while 2 percent are fluent in an Asian language. Tyson Fresh Meats, the area's largest employer, employs 5,256, and Beef Products Inc., BPI, has 250 employees. Both plants are unionized with UFCW.

The U.S. Census Bureau shows that in 2010 Nebraska's population was 9.2 percent Hispanic. The cities previously listed house the larger meatpacking plants in the state, where many of the

Latino workers are employed. According to the census, the Hispanic population in the cities number as follows: Schuyler, 65 percent; Lexington, 60 percent; South Sioux City, 45 percent; Grand Island, 27 percent; Columbus, 16 percent; and Fremont, 12 percent. According to the Pew report, the unauthorized immigrant populations in Nebraska approximated 5,000 in 1990; 30,000 in 2000; 45,000 in 2005; and 50,000 in 2007. In 2010 their numbers dipped to 45,000, and they made up 3 percent of the entire labor force and 2.4 percent of the population.

The number of Mexican workers in the Midwest has doubled since 1996, and in the 2000 census both Lexington and Schuyler's Hispanic populations had increased by 50 percent. Transnational migrations are changing the face of Nebraska cities as new immigrants abandon the struggling economies in their countries in search of better socioeconomic opportunities. However, in the author's view not much acknowledgment is given to the Latino presence on city websites or planning reports. The large growth in Latino inhabitants appears to be relegated to merely their meatpacking employment. Nonetheless, the Mayans interviewed engage in their own activism in a small but official way; they list their Mayan ethnicity in the "Other" category on the census to ensure they will somehow be acknowledged.

The bank manager invited me to take a look at the census information. It shows that the zero to seventeen year olds in the state of Nebraska are concentrated in the counties on the meatpacking loop on the eastern side of Nebraska. He smiled, stating, "Packing house towns have young men. And young men have children."[18] The Spanish language and Latinos have become a strong presence in Nebraskan cities near the meatpacking plants that dot the rural farmland.

The meatpacking towns have undergone rapid demographic, social, and economic tranformations.[19] The newcomers trigger a chain reaction that impacts many levels of civic life. The influx of new residents strains the educational system and other government services and augments social service demands that affect medical care providers and law enforcement agencies. Hispanics, as yet, are still outside the circle of community and political leadership. This remains a major source of conflict and challenge. Tax receipts can't cover the needs that the rapid population growth causes, although the tax base and property values are growing. Housing shortages spark increases in rent and home sales. Increased population rates augment the strain on health care services, and some towns experience a shortage of doctors. There's also a lack of Spanish-speaking reporters at local newspapers, and there are few newspapers in Spanish.

A local school superintendent guesses that 60 percent of the students' parents are working at the meatpacking plant. His district is 30 percent Caucasian and 70 percent Latino whereas twelve years ago it was 60 percent Caucasian and 40 percent Latino. The local K-12 school districts are especially affected by the burgeoning enrollments of Latino students. He reports it is now more vibrant and has a more global perspective. More students have required an increase in teaching staff. Teachers have to cope with the different languages the newcomers speak, and they struggle over the language issue with the parents. Everyone expresses the desire to work together in the community, and English is the much desired and needed tool to facilitate that.

The major issue the school system faces is the poverty that causes both parents to work. They use programs such as Head Start, Early Head Start, and Save the Children to identify at-risk students early on, most of whom come from impoverished families, and this is effective. The superintendent says, "This has to become our educational focus: Stopping the cycle of poverty!" The district seeks to identify preschoolers and their parents, and intervene early on. Approximately 70 percent of their students in his district receive free or reduced lunch at school. He says he has an exceptional team of educators, and he is thankful for the recent federal incentive dollars that helped them expand their facilities.

The Head Start office started out in a one-room office, but has had to expand into a new building four times as large, with two teachers for both the morning and afternoon sessions. The office secretary smiled, stating, "It just keeps on growing and growing." Social workers or teachers get together with families in their homes, to learn more about their actual living situation and find ways to help the parents educate their children best. Sometimes, they have seen six to seven families living in one house, with one family per room. Some individuals rent the houses by rooms although it may be illegal to do so, and a local charity gives them furniture. She explains they were accustomed to living in extended familial kinship clans in Guatemala, and they seek out the same here, even if there is no bloodline relationship. Of course, this creates a cultural conflict that could result in removal of the children if Child Protective Services is alerted. She laments how difficult it is to explain to them that in the United States children need to live alone with their parents in one home, not in these extended clan networks that are comforting to them and also facilitate economic survival.

Martha points out that the undocumented parents can apply for and attain benefits from WIC and Head Start, as well as free lunch and health and dental insurance, whereas documented Mayans are not eligible. This creates feelings of animosity. Martha continues: "And how must the native Nebraskans feel? Government officials need to answer to all these loopholes in the system so as to prevent racism and anti-immigrant feelings." But these programs continue their work in the community regardless of the inconsistencies. One Head Start employee reported, "The job we do is low wage, but higher earning."

The Head Start office also stresses the adverse poverty in their community, stating, "People need food!" She says some of the Guatemalans have started growing food and sharing it with others, taking up the practices from back home, and thus creating a new model. The religious institutions are also aware of this reality. In one city with more than fourteen congregations, each one takes a turn helping the poor with bills or by providing a food pantry, and another nearby meatpacking city has a mobile food pantry.

The city library has become a busy hub, and the librarians are enthusiastic about the services they provide. One shows us they now have a Spanish/English bilingual web page and states most of the recent newcomers are Somalis who speak Arabic. "They all bring newcomers to the library first, and we give them information regarding ESL and GED. We have computers and free internet access for them, as well as language materials for their use."

Referring to all the new arrivals, a local bank manager says, "It's not bad or good. It has just changed. It depends on how you look at it. Our city is 65 percent Hispanic, and the schools are 85 percent. Some don't embrace newcomers. I call it 'white fright,' not 'white flight.' They left our schools and now miss the opportunities for diversity." At the bank, 25 percent of his staff is bilingual, and the main mortgage lender graduated from a local high school and is bilingual. Many of the bilingual women working at the bank are young mothers, and he says working with all of them at the bank is delightful. He is proud of the professional staffing at the bank and states, "Bilingualism is very important for business nowadays." However, the business he has is not from the undocumented. In their kinship clans they know the undocumented cannot have bank accounts. Martha shares: "My husband kept María's sister's money in our account. He advised her not to send all the money she made to Guatemala, and then, when she was deported, she took all the money she had in the bank with her." In this way there is some extralegal "banking." The bank manager points out that as farms have grown, farm families have declined, causing local stores to close. He adds, "The town was changing either way." His main concern is the vibrancy of the police and school systems: "Education costs money; but so does ignorance." In observing community trends among the Latinos he notes they many are no longer renting, but are instead buying homes. He tells me Nebraska was first populated by the Irish, Czechs, Germans, and Polish. Now it is Latinos. One client asked him, "When are they going to fit in?," and he answered, "Probably never. We still have a Czech queen every year!"

The Mayans are a small but important part of the Latino immigrants who have arrived. Some are undocumented, and they have come in search of economic stability and a better daily life. Their main concern is familial values and sustenance. They want what's best for their children, worrying and fretting over their nutrition and education. They are exemplary mothers, putting children first, so that they, as individuals, will thrive and help make the planet a better place for all of society. Their dreams are basic, their characters profound, and their manner is dignified. The Mayan women in Nebraska would live and work anywhere, in any job, to ensure their children have a better life than they did struggling in poverty in Guatemala.

The Mayans reflect a global economic situation that forces people to migrate toward the wealth needed to merely live life with dignity and seek out a better life for their offspring. Martha and her husband prepare lovely steaks they buy at the plant with a discount, their additional freezer and fridge filled with meat, and we enjoy them as a family, all together around the table, and they are delicious. They appreciate having the meat and don't harbor negative sentiments about the conditions at the meatpacking plant. They accept that processing meat is just another part of the cyclical nature of life and sustenance on the planet. On some level we all have our place on the meatpacking assembly line; as cutters, packers, or consumers, we are all a part of this design for global living, consumerism, and survival on this shared planet.

Conclusion

The Mayans and the community members were more than willing to tell about their past and present situation living together in the meatpacking city, but at the end of each interview a personal vision for a more harmonious and egalitarian trilingual and tricultural future in their city always surfaced. The sheriff hopes to see more active Latino involvement in the community, stating: "They tend to stay to themselves, on the porch with their families. There are leaders, but we need more liaisons." The bank manager also expressed his concern that future leaders are fostered, as he wondered aloud who will step up to the plate. He concluded, "Hopefully the Latinos will." Community members would also like to see the Latinos pursue political involvement, have a presence on councils, and run for public office. They presently have a community forum to talk about the good things happening in their city, but one community member reported that unfortunately most of the Latinos feel they don't speak English well enough to participate.

Community members would also like to see Latino church involvement extend into the community, thus doing away with the separation between the newcomers and the natives living together in one city. Martha states the same: "In terms of religion, the social part is more important than the spiritual. We can't stay inside the church praying; we must get out into the community. What will our future be? Will there be Latino mayors, leaders, and politicians? Will we be prepared for leadership?"

One parent sees more integration in the big cities like Lexington and South Sioux City, but often the problem with smaller cities is that people isolate themselves from one another to a greater extent. However, the schools have done a fine job of integrating students' parents, by providing bilingual information, but since they rely on the children to communicate it to parents, it may never reach them. One parent stated she'd like to see immigrant parents become more involved in the children's music and sports activities. She felt they need to participate in football, volleyball, and basketball, in addition to soccer. She lamented that some parents complain that the Latinos just don't do anything, but another mother thinks they just need to ask them to participate. For example, the parents feed the football team one night a week before the games. When they finally asked one Latina mom to bring some food, she was so excited, stating she had always felt left out.

Some community members appreciate the arrival of the Mayans because they are revitalizing midwestern towns that were being abandoned, bringing in children and often buying and repairing homes whose desertion the elderly in the community had mourned, having raised their children in them. At the end of conversations with both Mayans and community members, it was obvious both had often pondered some idyllic futures for their shared community.

And how have the interviewees' lives changed since our conversations in 2005? Over the years Martha learned about the process of attaining U.S. citizenship and filed the papers. She is now a U.S. citizen. María mothered a little boy and little girl in Nebraska, making her own family to replace the one she missed so much back in Guatemala, and she now works in a local company. Lucía and Manuela's whereabouts are unknown.

By 2010 José was gone. Martha explained the work visa Father had helped him get to attend his mother's funeral wasn't so great after all. "It was year to year Anna. He had to try and renew it each year, to see if he could continue on here. That is so difficult too. So stressful. Just more insecurity as to what will happen next. Our future is never sound." And then his wife contracted an illness,

"A terminal one, Anna. She was dying." And so he left Nebraska and returned to Guatemala.

Juana managed to return to Guatemala and bring her two girls back to Nebraska to join her other two children and husband. Martha excitedly detailed: "She pretended to be a Mayan indigenous woman from Chiapas to cross the border between Guatemala and Mexico. She learned words in the Mayan language of that area, dressed in the *coyote's* wife's regional clothing, and rode over the border in his car with him and her two girls in the back seat, rather than crossing on foot. She even taught her two daughters to say 'mom' and 'dad' in the Mayan language." Once over the border, she returned the wife's *traje*, and the husband pushed a package of tamales into her hands when he bid her goodbye. She was very thankful for this homemade food, so far from home, savory sustenance for the grueling journey ahead. She now works at a local restaurant.

The Mayans have managed to continue etching out their transnational lives. Communities experiencing these migrations, either by losing residents who set out on foot or by receiving newcomers, exemplify our global society and its imposed interrelatedness, complete with all the inconsistencies and lack of organization in this ever-evolving process of life on the planet. All war has underlying economic motives; those who plan wars and those who suffer the consequences of war lie on two very different points on the spectrum of human rights for living and coexisting on this planet, and that spectrum needs to be questioned and realigned on a regular basis. And the United States will need to accomplish immigration reform. The Evangelical pastor stated: "We pray to God, that he will give reason to Obama, to the legislators, so that they will pass immigration reform and give everyone a driver's license."

Some of the Mayans continue working at the plant to secure their future while they await immigration reform. Each piece of meat that comes through their hands for slicing and preparation at the plant was raised on the corn from those fields Lucía observed when she first moved to Nebraska. The Mayans frequently utter the names of the Nebraska meatpacking plants with surprising ease and a Mayan- and Spanish-inflected accent: "Tyson, JBS, Swift, Hormel, Cargill, Excel." The names roll off their limited English-speaking tongues with an odd familiarity. The Mayans migrate for work, cutting Nebraska beef into steaks, providing the bulk for American sustenance. The agribusiness corporations that place the plants on the plains do so in an effort to stimulate local economies, but as with any business, not all of the outcomes are or can be either predicted or planned for. This is what creates the present-day reality the women live, as they weave in and out of new lands and cultures, workplace policies, immigration documentation requirements, and host community responses to their presence, inventing a new Mayan-Nebraskan identity.

They now live somewhere between two countries and three cultures. According to Martha, "When we return to Guatemala, to our homeland, they call us 'grindios,' combining the words 'gringo' and 'indios' or Indians, due to the fact that we live in the U.S., among the americanos. They now associate us with this country, and therefore with its policies?! But in our hearts we are still Mayans."

On December 21, 2012, the Mayan calendar rolled to the end of a more than 5,000-year cycle of time. Martha gently explained that many Westerners perceive time with a beginning and an end, but that "Mayans see time as circular, not linear." She hopes humanity will heed the circular nature of the Mayan calendar, taking care not to wear the planet out by always taking more than one needs. The results of global warming are readily apparent, and we must recall the planet is the future home for our children. Martha states: "If we can consider time as cyclical, and that all is interrelated and moves in a never-ending circle, possibly it would allow for more planning that takes into consideration all members of the global community." Many Mayans share this knowledge and hope about the cyclical nature of time and the need to observe and watch after each part of the whole of our planet. We encourage you, dear reader, to read Kaqla's work, *La palabra y el sentir de las Mujeres Mayas de Kaqla* (The word and feelings of the Mayan women of Kaqla). It provides an exemplary vision for a just, joyful, democratic, inclusive society that transforms daily life and promotes equality among all people, regardless of gender or ethnicity, doing so with respect for diversity and the self-determination of all peoples, in harmony with nature. We also encourage you to watch *2012: The Mayan Word* on YouTube, to hear Mayans talking about their reflections on the past and their vision for life in this new cycle.

The Mayan women interviewed in Nebraska have handed over their personal stories to you, dear reader, to increase communication and understanding between all people living in Guatemala, the United States, and on earth. They hope that they have touched your heart, and your personal experience of life on this planet, and that you will somehow see your connection to them, their homeland, and their stories in their new land, which may also be your land. Our vision for the future must be one of working together for the well-being of all, and as stated in the Rigoberta Menchú quote in the introduction, we must recall that each of us is merely one tiny kernel on the ear of corn of life.

Notes

Preface

1. All words used in Spanish are placed in italics, defined in the text, and included in the glossary.

2. The *Popol Vuh*, the Quich'e Mayan book of creation, includes the word *pop* in its title. *Popol* had the meaning of "public," or "in common," and the verb *popoj* meant "to hold a council." "*Popol*, literally 'partaking of a mat,' is a metonym for a council, referring to the mat on which its members sat; at the same time it might have been a metaphor for the way councils were structured, weaving diverse interests together" (Tedlock, *Popol Vuh*, 218).

Introduction

1. Ladino is a Guatemalan term referring to mestizos, people of Spanish and indigenous descent who speak Spanish (see chapter 2 for further explanation).

2. "St. Benedict had that wonderful vision in which he came as near to seeing God as is possible for man in this life. St. Gregory and St. Bonaventure say that Benedict saw God and in that vision of God saw the whole world." See Ford, "St. Benedict of Nursia," http://www.newadvent.org/.

3. Menchú, *Rigoberta: La nieta de los mayas*, 163. All English translations are the authors'.

1. Guatemala

1. See Grupo de Mujeres Mayas Kaqla, *La palabra y el sentir*, 62–63, 66, 71–73, and 78–79, for a detailed discussion regarding Mayan language groups and the attitudes about how language or clothing relates to identity. As well, Menchú, *Rigoberta: La nieta de los mayas*, 86, 215, 284, 334–35, notes the need to explore self-identity and self-worth from within the culture; language as patrimony and a part of nature and the Mayan universe; the meetings held around the Fifth Centenary of the "discovery" of the Americas at which indig-

enous people noted their shared experience over the past five hundred years; the way the military divided Mayans by ethnicity in order to conquer them; and the fact that not speaking the same language and having to learn Spanish has been divisive for them.

2. Molesky-Poz, *Contemporary Mayan Spirituality*, 50–52.

3. Menchú, *Rigoberta: La nieta de los mayas*, 324.

4. Velásquez Nimatuj, "Transnationalism and Maya Dress," 529.

5. "Mayan Pupils Allowed to Wear Traditional Attire," *New York Times*, April 8, 1997, A5.

6. Velásquez Nimatuj, "Transnationalism and Maya Dress," 528.

7. See Grupo de Mujeres Mayas Kaqla, *La palabra y el sentir*, 54–83, for a discussion regarding the many levels of meaning behind wearing the *traje*, speaking their languages, and reconstructing a Mayan identity from within.

8. Grupo de Mujeres Mayas Kaqla, *La palabra y el sentir*, 77.

9. Menchú and Burgos-Debray, *I, Rigoberta Menchú: An Indian Woman*, 82.

10. Menchú and Burgos-Debray, *I, Rigoberta Menchú: An Indian Woman*, 82.

11. Menchú and Burgos-Debray, *I, Rigoberta Menchú: An Indian Woman*, 83.

2. Guatemalan Civil War and Postwar Rebuilding

1. For a detailed synopsis of the Guatemalan civil war and U.S. involvement, see Comisión para el Esclarecimiento Histórico, *Guatemala Memoria*, 19–20; Grandin et al., *Guatemala Reader*, 3–7; Gonzalez, *Harvest of Empire*, 135–38; Schlesinger and Kinzer, *Bitter Fruit*; Zinn, *A People's History of the United States*, 439. Regarding the United Fruit Company and U.S. interest in it, see Schlesinger and Kinzer, *Bitter Fruit*, 65–118.

2. Literally, killed by the military.

3. See Comisión para el Esclarecimiento, *Guatemala Memoria*, 38, 44. The report states the Guatemalan army illegally forced thousands of young people to join forces and participate in hostilities, employing forced recruitment that was discriminatory in nature against the Mayan population and included young people under the age of fifteen, a violation of their personal liberty.

4. Menchú and Burgos-Debray, *I, Rigoberta Menchú: An Indian Woman*, 167.

5. Comisión para el Esclarecimiento, *Guatemala Memoria*, 19.

6. See Comisión para el Esclarecimiento, *Guatemala Memoria*, 27, 35–36. Also González Izás, "Arbitrary Power and Sexual Violence," in Grandin et al., 405–10, for an explanation of the way rape was construed as "taking," "using," or "appropriating the enemy's women" and employed as a central part of the repressive actions of the army and the civil patrol.

7. "Enjuician a militares por masacre en Guatemala," *La Nación*, Costa Rica,

Grupo Nación GN, July 26, 2011, http://www.nacion.com/ 2011–07–26/Mundo
/enjuician-a-militares-por-masacre-en-guatemala.aspx.

8. Comisión para el Esclarecimiento, *Guatemala Memoria*, 28.

9. John M. Broder, "Clinton Offers His Apologies," *New York Times*, March 11,
1999, http://www.nytimes.com/1999/03/11/world/clinton-offers-his-apologies
-to-guatemala.html.

10. "Sangría en Guatemala," Editorial, *La Nación*, July 17, 2011, A26.

11. See Chomsky, *Class Warfare*.

12. United Nations, *Charter of the United Nations and Statute of the International Court of Justice*.

3. The Journey to El Norte

1. Amnesty International, "Migrants Making Dangerous Journey through
Mexico 'Desperately Need Socks,'" Amnesty International News, January 26, 2012,
http://www.amnestyusa.org/news/press-releases/migrants-making-dangerous
-journey-through-mexico-desperately-need-socks-says-amnesty-international.
Also, see Nazario, *Enrique's Journey*, which details the violent, senseless attacks
on child immigrants crossing Mexico on top of trains to search for the parents who left them behind to migrate to El Norte in search of economic stability for their families.

2. Amnesty International, "Migrants Making Dangerous Journey."

3. Amnesty International, "Migrants Making Dangerous Journey."

4. IOM, "Guatemala."

5. IOM, "Guatemala," 91.

6. IOM, "Guatemala," 79.

7. Minority Rights Group International, *World Directory – Guatemala*.

8. The border-crossing reality and undocumented immigrant situation
has been depicted in numerous films such as *Who is Dayani Cristal?*; *Documented: A Film by an ~~illegal immigrant~~ undocumented American; Sin país; Sin
nombre; El alambrista; Dying to Get In; La Misma Luna; Trade; Crossing Arizona*; and *Which Way Home*.

9. Travel.State.Gov, A Service of the Bureau of Consular Affairs, "U.S. Visa
Policy," Bureau of Consular Affairs, U.S. Department of State, accessed July
20, 2012, http:// travel.state.gov/ visa/questions/policy/policy_4433.html.

10. There are many types of visas for legally permitted travel to the United
States such as: B2 Visitor, B1 Business, K1 Fiancé, F1 Student, J1 Visitor Exchange,
H1B Work, H2A Temporary Agricultural Workers, H2B Temporary or Seasonal
Workers, H3 Trainee, L1 Intracompany Transferee Visas. Application fees for
a Tourist, Business, Transit, Crew Member, Student, Exchange Visitor, and
Journalist visas from Guatemala are $160 and for Petition-Based visas (H, L,

O, P, Q, and R), $190. All visas vary on the amount of time granted and the application processes. See Travel.State.Gov for a complete listing of immigrant and visitor visas.

11. Foner, *Across Generations*, 2–3.

12. "The Last Word: West Coast Writers and Artists," *Zyzzyva*, 2012, http://www.zyzzyva.org/2012/08/01/from-iguala-to-los-angeles-the-making-of-a-writer-qa-with-reyna-grande/.

13. Nazario, *Enrique's Journey*, xxv. Nazario states: "[M]y hope is that they will understand the full consequences of leaving their children behind and make better-informed decisions. For in the end, these separations almost always end badly. Every woman I interviewed in the United States who had left children behind had been sure the separation would be brief. Immigrants who come to the United States are by nature optimists. They have to be in order to leave everything they love and are familiar with for the unknown. The reality, however, is that it takes years and years until the children and mothers are together again. By the time that happens, if it happens, the children are usually very angry with their mothers. They feel abandoned. Their mothers are stunned by this judgment. They believe their children should show gratitude, not anger. After all, the mothers sacrificed being with their children, worked like dogs, all to help provide their children with a better life and future."

14. Nazario, *Enrique's Journey*, 101.

15. Anna O. Law, "Lies, Damned Lies, and Obama's Deportation Statistics," *The Washington Post*, April 21, 2014, http:// www.washingtonpost.com/blogs/monkeycage/wp/2014/04/21/lies-damned-lies-and-obamas-deportation-statistics/.

16. Brian Bennett, "High Deportation Figures Are Misleading," *Los Angeles Times*, April 1, 2014, http://www.latimes.com/nation/la-na-obama-deportations-20140402-story.html#page=1.

17. Nelsen, "Torn Apart."

18. See Nelsen, "Torn Apart," Wheeler, *Between Light and Shadow*, and *Discovering Dominga* for transnational examples of children who ended up in state custody or were given up for adoption after parents were deported or labeled unfit to parent by discriminatory policies because of language limitations or because their home environment in their country of origin was deemed less than beneficial.

4. Religious Practice and Community Life in Nebraska

1. Molesky-Poz, *Mayan Spirituality*, 59.

2. See Molesky-Poz, *Mayan Spirituality*, 1–2, 16–20, for a detailed account of the changes in religion in Guatemala.

3. Zur, *Violent Memories*, 31.

4. Zur, *Violent Memories*, 39.

5. Comisión para el Esclarecimiento, *Guatemala Memoria*, 20.

6. The Pew Forum on Religion and Public Life, "Christianity and Conflict in Latin America."

7. Molesky-Poz, *Mayan Spirituality*, 21.

8. Molesky-Poz, *Mayan Spirituality*, 22.

9. Minority Rights Group International, *World Directory – Guatemala*.

10. *Program Pastoral Mayan*, 7.

11. Immigration Policy Center, "Violence Against Women Act (VAWA) Provides Protections for Immigrant Women and Victims of [sic]," American Immigration Council, May 7, 2012, http:// www.immigrationpolicy.org/just-facts /misplaced-priorities-most-immigrants-deported-ice-2013-were-threat-no-one.

12. Nebraska Corn Board, "Nebraska Corn Production and Uses," accessed July 24, 2012, http://www.nebraskacorn.org/. See also Pollan, *Omnivore's Dilemma*, 1–119, for an overview of the history of corn, its overproduction and overconsumption in the United States, how that has affected feed and meat production, consumption, and exportation, and the role large meatpacking plants play in our industrial food chain, agricultural policy, and the global market.

5. Mayans and Meatpacking in Nebraska

1. "Nebraska Beef Goes Global."

2. "Nebraska Beef Goes Global."

3. See Dalla and Christensen, "Latino Immigrants Describe Residence," 23–42; Dalla, Cramer, and Stanek, "Economic Strain and Community," 20– 25; Fink, *Cutting into the Meatpacking Line*; Fink and Dunn, *The Maya of Morganton*; Gouveia and Saenz, "Global Forces and Latino Population Growth," 305–28; Gouveia and Stull, *Latino Immigrants, Meatpacking, and Rural Communities*; Popkin, "Guatemalan Mayan Migration to Los Angeles," 238–66; Rochín, "Latinos on the Great Plains," 243–52; Stanley, "Immigrant and Refugee Workers in the Midwestern Meatpacking Industry," 106–17; Stull and Broadway, *Slaughterhouse Blues*; and Stull, Broadway, and Griffith, *Any Way You Cut It*, for detailed research on the interrelationship between meatpacking plants, Latino workers, and immigration policy.

4. Nebraska Beef Council, "State/National Facts," 2010.

5. U.S. Department of Agriculture, "Cattle and Beef," October 31, 2013.

6. Lopez, Gonzalez-Barrera, and Motel, "As Deportations Rise."

7. In 2010, voters in Fremont approved (by 57 percent) an ordinance denying employment and housing to undocumented immigrants, but it was appealed by the Nebraska ACLU and a federal judge struck part of it down in 2012. In

2013 a federal appeals panel upheld the city's ban. In January 2010 state senator Janssen of Fremont introduced the Illegal Immigration Enforcement Act. In Nebraska in April 2009, a prenatal care proposal for pregnant undocumented women was defeated.

8. "INS Questions Nebraska Meatpacking Workers as Part of Operation Vanguard."

9. For more details, see "125 Arrested in Nebraska Immigration Raid," *New York Times*, March 5, 1995, as well as Compa, *Blood, Sweat, and Fear*, 113.

10. Ted Conover, "The Way of All Flesh: Undercover in an Industrial Slaughterhouse," *Harper's Magazine*, May 2013, 31–49; Justin Pritchard, "Dying to Work in El Norte," *Lincoln Journal Star*, March 13, 2004, http://www.journalstar.com/. See also "The Speed Kills You," for further discussion regarding safety issues in the meatpacking plants.

11. Compa, *Blood, Sweat, and Fear*, 60.

12. See Conover, "The Way of All Flesh," and Schlosser, *Fast Food Nation* for an overview of meatpacking plants and pointed questions about the working conditions therein.

13. "The Speed Kills You," 27.

14. Compa, *Blood, Sweat, and Fear*, 14.

15. IOM, "Guatemala," 17.

16. Smith, *Guatemala: Economic Migrants Replace Political Refugees*.

17. Schlosser uses the term "Mexington," in *Fast Food Nation*, 165. All data regarding population and employment at the plants is from Nebraska Public Power District, Economic Development Department, "A Nebraska Public Power District Service, Nebraska Community Fast Facts Profile," econdev.nppd.com.

18. See Ennis, Ríos-Vargas, and Albert, "The Hispanic Population: 2010."

19. See Broadway, "Meatpacking and the Transformation of Rural Communities," and "Planning for Change in Small Towns"; Champlin and Hake, "Immigration as an Industrial Strategy"; Dalla and Christensen, "Latino Immigrants Describe Residence"; Dalla, Cramer, and Stanek, "Economic Strain and Community"; Fink, *Cutting into the Meatpacking Line*; Fink and Dunn, *The Maya of Morganton*; Gouveia and Saenz, "Global Forces and Latino Population Growth"; Gouveia and Stull, *Latino Immigrants, Meatpacking, and Rural Communities*; Popkin, "Guatemalan Mayan Migration to Los Angeles"; Rochín, "Latinos on the Great Plains"; Stanley, "Immigrant and Refugee Workers in the Midwestern Meatpacking Industry"; Stull and Broadway, *Slaughterhouse Blues*; and Stull, Broadway, and Griffith, in *Any Way You Cut It*, for research on the effects that newcomer immigrant worker populations have on local communities with meatpacking plants.

Glossary

achiote: a shrub seed used to give food red coloring.
americanos: Americans.
apazote: an herb similar to cilantro; American basil.
atol: a drink made from corn flour.
Ay: Oh my! Expresses pain, threat, fear, or pity.
Banco de Guatemala: the Bank of Guatemala.
berros: watercress.
el charro: Mexican cowboy.
chile: hot peppers.
chuj: Mayan Mam word for an adobe structure housing a Mayan sauna and bath.
cinta: a Mayan woven sash used to roll up one's hair.
comal: a flat, wrought-iron griddle for heating tortillas.
Comisión de Esclarecimiento Histórico (CEH): Guatemalan Commission for Historical Clarification. It was established through the Oslo Accords in 1994.
comunidad: community.
corte: a Mayan woven skirt.
costumbre: or Custom, is a Mayan religious practice in which brotherhoods are organized in a hierarchical structure led by elders; they plan and raise money within the community to finance religious celebrations and processions, usually for saints.
coyote: person who provides the service of border crossing for a fee.
dialecto: literally, "dialect," and the way many people in

Guatemala refer to the more than twenty Mayan indigenous languages.

El Norte: The North or the United States.

fiesta or feria: town festival, celebration, or religious festival.

gringo: the term used in Guatemala to refer to a person of U.S. nationality.

guerrilla, guerrilleros: guerrilla insurgency fighters.

hierba: greens or herbs.

hierba mora: mint.

huipil: a Mayan woven blouse.

indio: Indian.

Ladino: a Guatemalan term referring to mestizos, people of Spanish and indigenous descent who speak Spanish.

limpieza: cleansing.

machista: male chauvinist society.

masa: corn meal dough for making tortillas.

la milpa: corn or cornfields.

mostaza: mustard greens.

la muerte: death.

nabo: turnip greens.

nixtamal: corn masa for making tortillas.

patrulleros: civil patrol officers.

pop: Mayan word for partaking of the mat, or participating in councils.

Popol Vuh: the Mayan book of creation.

profesora: teacher; instructor.

quetzal: Guatemalan national bird.

quetzales: Guatemalan monetary unit.

remesas: remittances.

sauco: also called *chilca,* a plant with cleansing properties.

señora: title for a married woman, an older woman, or the female head of a household.

tacos de lengua: tongue tacos.

tortilla: flat corn patty.

traje: the Mayan clothing that varies according to indigenous ethnic regions and language groups; Mayan women wear a woven blouse or *huipil* and a woven skirt or *corte*.

trapear: mop or wash the floor.

triste: sad.

vaqueros: cowboys.

zacate: hay, or dry grass or plants.

Bibliography

"2012: The Mayan Word" (film). Directed by Melissa Gunasena. http://2012 mayanword.blogspot.com/. Accessed October 30, 2013.

Alambrista Emplumado: The Fence Jumper (film). Directed by Alfonso Sahagun Casaus. New York: BrinkDVD, 2008. DVD.

Banco de Guatemala. "Ingreso de Divisas por Remesas Familiares" [Foreign currency income due to familial remittances]. *Banco de Guatemala.* http://www.banguat.gob.gt/. Accessed March 24, 2012.

Broadway, Michael J. "Meatpacking and the Transformation of Rural Communities: A Comparison of Brooks, Alberta, and Garden City, Kansas." *Rural Sociology* 72, no. 4 (2007): 560–82.

———. "Planning for Change in Small Towns or Trying to Avoid the Slaughterhouse Blues." *Journal of Rural Studies* 16, no. 1 (2000): 37–46.

Caballeros, Álvaro. "Perfil Migratorio de Guatemala 2012" [Guatemalan migratory profile 2012]. *Organización Internacional para las Migraciones (OIM).* http://publications.iom.int/bookstore/free/MPGuatemala_11july2013 .pdf. Accessed November 20, 2013.

Camarota, Steven A. "Immigrants in the United States, 2010: A Profile of America's Foreign-Born Population." *Center for Immigration Studies.* http://www.cis.org/2012-profile-of-americas-foreign-born-population#birth. Accessed November 20, 2013.

Champlin, Dell, and Eric Hake. "Immigration as an Industrial Strategy in American Meatpacking." *Review of the Political Economy* 18, no. 1 (2006): 49–69.

Chomsky, Noam. *Class Warfare: Interviews with David Barsamian.* Monroe MD: Common Courage, 1996.

Coe, Michael D. *The Maya.* New York: Thames and Hudson, 2011.

Comisión para el Esclarecimiento Histórico (Guatemala). *Guatemala Memoria del Silencio: Tz'inil Na'tab'al. Conclusiones y Recomendaciones del Informe de la Comisión para el Esclarecimiento Histórico* [Guatemala: Memory of Silence. Report of the Commission for Historical Clarification. Conclusions and Recommendations]. Guatemala: CEH, between 1998 and 2000. http://shr.aaas.org/guatemala/ceh/mds/spanish/.

Compa, Lance A. *Blood, Sweat, and Fear: Workers' Rights in U.S. Meat and Poultry Plants*. New York: Human Rights Watch, 2004.

Crossing Arizona (film). Directed by Joseph Mathew, Dan DeVivo, Laurie MacMillan, and Byrd Baylor. New York: Rainlake Productions, 2008. DVD.

Cu, Maya. *La rueda* [The Wheel]. Guatemala: Editorial Cultura, 2002.

Cu, Maya, Juan Carlos Lemus, Alfonso Porres, Fernando Ramos, and Emilio Solano. *Novísimos* [Newest Ones]. Guatemala: Editorial Cultura, 1996.

Dalla, Rochelle L., and April Christensen. "Latino Immigrants Describe Residence in Rural Midwestern Meatpacking Communities: A Longitudinal Assessment of Social and Economic Change." *Hispanic Journal of Behavioral Sciences* 27, no. 1 (2005): 23–42.

Dalla, Rochelle L., Sheran Cramer, and Kaye Stanek. "Economic Strain and Community Concerns in Three Meatpacking Communities." *Rural America* 17, no. 1 (2002): 20–25.

Discovering Dominga (film). Directed by Patricia Flynn and Mary J. McConahay. Berkeley: University of California Extension Center for Media and Independent Learning, 2002. DVD.

Documented: A Film by an Illegal Immigrant Undocumented American (film). Directed by Jose Antonio Vargas. USA: Apo Anak Productions, 2014. DVD.

Dying to Get In: Illegal Immigration to the EU (film). NY: Films Media Group, 2005. DVD.

Ennis, Sharon R, Merarys Ríos-Vargas, and Nora G. Albert. "The Hispanic Population: 2010. 2010 Census Briefs." *U.S. Census Bureau. U.S. Department of Commerce, Economics and Statistics Administration*. May 2011. http://www.census.gov/ prod/cen2010/briefs/c2010br-04.pdf.

Fink, Deborah. *The Meatpacking Line: Workers and Change in the Rural Midwest*. Chapel Hill: University of North Carolina Press, 1998.

Fink, Leon, and Alvis E. Dunn. *The Maya of Morganton: Work and Community in the Nuevo New South*. Chapel Hill: University of North Carolina Press, 2003.

Foner, Nancy. *Across Generations: Immigrant Families in America*. New York: New York University Press, 2009.

Ford, Hugh. "St. Benedict of Nursia." In *New Advent: The Catholic Encyclopedia*. Vol. 2. Kevin Knight, 2012. http://www.newadvent.org/.

Freidel, David, Linda Schele, and Joy Parker. *Maya Cosmos: Three Thousand Years on the Shaman's Path*. New York: HarperCollins, 1993.

Gabriel Xiquín, Calixta. "Ausencia de madre/A Mother's Absence." In *Tejiendo los sucesos en el tiempo / Weaving Events in Time*, 56–57. CA: Yax Te' Foundation, 2002.

Gonzalez, Juan. *Harvest of Empire: A History of Latinos in America.* New York: Viking, 2000.

González Izás, Matilde. "Arbitrary Power and Sexual Violence." In *The Guatemala Reader: History, Culture, Politics,* edited by Greg Grandin, Deborah T. Levenson, and Elizabeth Oglesby, 405–10. Durham NC: Duke University Press, 2011.

Gouveia, Lourdes, and Rogelio Saenz. "Global Forces and Latino Population Growth in the Midwest: A Regional and Subregional Analysis." *Great Plains Research* 10 (2000): 305–28.

Gouveia, Lourdes, and Donald D. Stull. *Latino Immigrants, Meatpacking, and Rural Communities: A Case Study of Lexington, Nebraska.* East Lansing: Julian Samora Research Institute, Michigan State University, 1997.

Grande, Reyna. *The Distance between Us: A Memoir.* New York: Atria, 2012.

Grandin, Greg, Deborah Levenson-Estrada, and Elizabeth Oglesby. *The Guatemala Reader: History, Culture, Politics.* Durham NC: Duke University Press, 2011.

Grün, Anselm. *Mary Fruit of New Creation.* Schuyler NE: Benedict Press, 2001.

Grupo de Mujeres Mayas Kaqla. *La palabra y el sentir de las Mujeres Mayas de Kaqla* [The word and feelings of the Mayan women of Kaqla]. Guatemala: Grupo de Mujeres Mayas Kaqla, 2004.

Immigration Policy Center. "Misplaced Priorities: Most Immigrants Deported by ICE in 2013 Were a Threat to No One." American Immigration Council, March 28, 2014. http://www.immigrationpolicy.org/just-facts /misplaced-priorities-most-immigrants-deported-ice-2013-were-threat -no-one.

———."Violence Against Women Act (VAWA) Provides Protections for Immigrant Women and Victims of [*sic*]". American Immigration Council, May 7, 2012. http://www.immigrationpolicy.org/just-facts/misplaced-priorities -most-immigrants-deported-ice-2013-were-threat-no-one.

"INS Questions Nebraska Meatpacking Workers as Part of Operation Vanguard." *Immigrants' Rights Update* 13, no. 3 (May 28, 1999). http://140.174.87.56 /immsemplymnt/ wkplce_enfrcmnt/wkplcenfrc008.htm.

IOM: International Organization for Migration. "Guatemala: Facts and Figures." November 2013. http://www.iom.int/cms/en/sites/iom/home/where-we -work/americas/central- and-north-america- and-th/guatemala.html.

La Jaula De Oro [The golden dream] (film). Directed by Diego Quemada-Díez. Amsterdam: Wild Bunch Benelux Distribution, 2014. DVD.

La Misma Luna. Under the Same Moon (film). Directed by Patricia Riggen. Beverly Hills CA: 20th Century Fox Home Entertainment, 2008. DVD.

Lopez, Mark Hugo, Ana Gonzalez-Barrera, and Seth Motel. "As Deportations Rise to Record Levels, Most Latinos Oppose Obama's Policy." *Pew*

Research Center. Pew Hispanic Center. December 28, 2011. http://www
.pewhispanic.org/2011/12/28/ appendix-a-deportations-reported-by-ice/.
Menchú, Rigoberta. *Rigoberta: La nieta de los mayas* [Rigoberta: Granddaugh-
ter of the Mayans]. Madrid: Grupo Santillana de Ediciones/Ediciones
El País, 1998.
Menchú, Rigoberta, and Elisabeth Burgos-Debray. *I, Rigoberta Menchú: An
Indian Woman in Guatemala.* London: Verso, 1984.
Minority Rights Group International. *World Directory of Minorities and Indige-
nous Peoples–Guatemala: Maya.* July 2008. http://www.unhcr.org/refworld
/docid/49749d163c.html.
Molesky-Poz, Jean. *Contemporary Mayan Spirituality.* Austin: University of
Texas Press, 2006.
National Poverty Center. Gerald R. Ford School of Public Policy, University of
Michigan, 2011. http://www.npc.umich.edu/.
Nazario, Sonia. *Enrique's Journey: The Story of a Boy's Dangerous Odyssey to
Reunite with his Mother.* New York: Random House, 2006.
Nebraska Beef Council. "State/National Facts." 2010. http:// www.nebeef.org
/statenationalfacts.aspx.
Nebraska Corn Board. "Nebraska Corn Production and Uses." http://www
.nebraskacorn.org/. Accessed July 24, 2012.
Nebraska Educational Telecommunications, Nebraska State Department of
Education, and Nebraska State Historical Society. "Nebraska Beef Goes
Global: Hispanic Migrations." http://www.nebraskastudies.org. Accessed
February 7, 2012.
Nebraska Public Power District. Economic Development Department. "A
Nebraska Public Power District Service. Nebraska Community Fast Facts
Profile." http://sites.nppd.com/default.aspx. Accessed November 24, 2013.
Nelsen, Aaron. "Torn Apart: How the Government Separates Parents and Chil-
dren." *In These Times: With Liberty and Justice for All.* December 20, 2011.
http://inthesetimes.com/article/12424/torn_apart_how_the_federal
_government_separates_parents_and_children.
Passel, Jeffrey, and D'Vera Cohn. "Unauthorized Immigrant Population:
National and State Trends." *Pew Research Center.* Pew Hispanic Center.
February 1, 2011. http://www.pewhispanic.org/2011/02/01/unauthorized
-immigrant-population-brnational- and-state-trends-2010/.
Passel, Jeffrey, D'Vera Cohn, and Mark Hugo Lopez. "Hispanics Account for More
Than Half of Nation's Growth in Past Decade." *Pew Research Center.* Pew His-
panic Center. March 24, 2011. http://www.pewhispanic.org/2011/03/24
/hispanics-account-for-more-than-half-of-nations-growth-in-past-decade/.
The Pew Forum on Religion and Public Life. "Christianity and Conflict in Latin
America." April 6, 2006. Washington D C: Event Transcript National Defense

University, 2010. http://www.pewforum.org/Government/Christianity
-and-Conflict-in-Latin-America.aspx.

Pollan, Michael. *The Omnivore's Dilemma: A Natural History of Four Meals.*
New York: Penguin, 2006.

Popkin, Eric. "Guatemalan Mayan Migration to Los Angeles: Constructing
Transnational Linkages in the Context of the Settlement Process." *Ethnic and Racial Studies* 22, no. 2 (1999): 238–66.

Program Pastoral Mayan. Pastoral Mayan National Leadership Conference.
Omaha NE: Archdiocese of Omaha, Creighton University, 2010.

Rochín, R. I. "Latinos on the Great Plains: An Overview." *Great Plains Research*
10 (2000): 243–52.

Save the Children Federation, Inc. "Save the Children: Guatemala." 2013.
http://www.savethechildren.org/site/ c.8rKLIXMGIpi4e/b.6151425/.

Schlesinger, Stephen C., and Stephen Kinzer. *Bitter Fruit: The Story of the American Coup in Guatemala.* Cambridge MA: Harvard University, David Rock-
efeller Center for Latin American Studies, 2005.

Schlosser, Eric. *Fast Food Nation: The Dark Side of the All-American Meal.* New
York: Perennial, 2002.

Sin Nombre [Without a name] (film). Directed by Cary J Fukunaga. Universal
City CA: Universal Studios Home Entertainment, 2009. DVD.

Sin País [Without a country] (film). Directed by Theo Rigby. Harriman NY:
New Day Films, 2010. DVD.

Smith, James. *Guatemala: Economic Migrants Replace Political Refugees.* Migration
Policy Institute. Migration Information Source. Inforpress Centroameri-
cana. April 2006. http://www.migrationinformation.org/feature/display
.cfm?ID=392.

"The Speed Kills You: The Voice of Nebraska's Meatpacking Workers." *Nebraska
Appleseed,* February 24, 2011. http:// neappleseed.org/immigrants.

Stanley, Kathleen. "Immigrant and Refugee Workers in the Midwestern Meatpacking Industry: Industrial Restructuring and the Transformation of
Rural Labor Markets." *Policy Studies Review* 11, no. 2 (1992): 106–17.

Stull, Donald D., and Michael J. Broadway. *Slaughterhouse Blues: The Meat
and Poultry Industry in North America.* Belmont CA: Wadworth Cen-
gage Learning, 2013.

Stull, Donald D., Michael J. Broadway, and David C. Griffith. *Any Way You
Cut It: Meat Processing and Small-Town America.* Lawrence: University
Press of Kansas, 1995.

Tedlock, Dennis, trans. *Popol Vuh: The Mayan Book of the Dawn of Life.* New
York: Simon and Schuster, 1996.

Trade (film). Directed by Marco Kreuzpaintner. Santa Monica CA: Lions-
gate, 2007. DVD.

Travel.State.Gov. A Service of the Bureau of Consular Affairs. "U.S. Visa Policy." Bureau of Consular Affairs, U.S. Department of State. http:// travel.state .gov/visa/questions/policy/policy_4433.html. Accessed July 20, 2012.

U.S. Census Bureau. "State and County QuickFacts." January 17, 2012. http:// quickfacts.census.gov/qfd/index.html.

U.S. Department of Agriculture, Economic Research Service. "Cattle and Beef." October 31, 2013. http://www.ers.usda.gov/topics/animal-products /cattle-beef/statistics-information.aspx.

U.S. Department of Homeland Security. "FY 2013 ICE Immigration Removals. Annual Report." Accessed June 4, 2014. http://www.ice.gov/doclib/about /offices/ero/pdf/2013-ice-immigration-removals.pdf.

U.S. Department of Homeland Security. U.S. Citizenship and Immigration Services. Accessed October 24, 2013. http://www.uscis.gov/portal/site /uscis.

U.S. Department of Labor, Bureau of Labor Statistics. "Occupational Employment and Wages, Slaughterers and Meat Packers." May 2010. http://www.bls .gov/ oes/current/ oes513023.htm#st.

U.S. Environmental Protection Agency. "Ag 101: Demographics." EPA Ag. Center. April 14, 2013. http://www.epa.gov/oecaagct/ag101/demographics .html.

The United Nations. Department of Public Information. *Charter of the United Nations and Statute of the International Court of Justice.* http://www.un.org/en /documents/charter/. Accessed January 9, 2012.

Velásquez Nimatuj, Irma Alicia. "Transnationalism and Maya Dress." In *The Guatemala Reader: History, Culture, Politics,* edited by Greg Grandin, Deborah T. Levenson, and Elizabeth Oglesby, 523–31. Durham NC: Duke University Press, 2011.

Wheeler, Jacob. *Between Light and Shadow: A Guatemalan Girl's Journey through Adoption.* Lincoln: University of Nebraska Press, 2011.

Which Way Home (film). Directed by Rebecca Cammisa. New York: Docurama, 2010. DVD.

Who Is Dayani Cristal? (film). Directed by Gael García Bernal and Marc Silver. New York: Kino Lorber, Inc., 2013. DVD.

The World Bank. *Report: Guatemala. Poverty Assessment. Good Performance at Low Levels.* March 18, 2009. http://siteresources.worldbank.org / INTLACREGTOPPOVANA/Resources/GuatemalaPovertyAssessment English.pdfReport No.43920-GT.

The World Bank Group. "The World Bank: Working for a World Free of Poverty." 2012. http://data.worldbank.org/country/guatemala.

World Health Organization. *Guatemala: Socioeconomic Context.* 2011. http://www
.who.int/substance_abuse/publications/global_alcohol_report/profiles
/gtm.pdf

Zinn, Howard. *A People's History of the United States, 1492–Present.* New York:
HarperCollins, 2003.

Zur, Judith N. *Violent Memories: Mayan War Widows in Guatemala.* Boulder
CO: Westview, 1998.

Index

interviews, xix–xxi, xviii; language and, xix; with non-immigrant community members, xxi

Ixchel, 7

JBS Swift, 130

José, xx, xxiii, 33–42, 49–50, 51; Ann meeting, 40–41; civil war experiences of, 27, 29, 33–42, 43; on divided families, 77–78, 89; on documentation, 67–68, 138–39; family of, 36, 40, 67–68; on gender inequity, 49–50; illnesses and injuries of, 34, 35–36, 37; on language, 18, 103; on local community, 96–97; on religious faith, 77, 78; on *remesas*, 94–95; returning to Guatemala, 138–39

Juana, xx; Ann mothering, 82–83; on anti-immigrant sentiment, 121; on civil war, 28; early life of, 8–9, 13, 17–18; on education, 18; family of, in U.S., 139; on food, 11–12, 93; on gender inequity, 17–18; on immigrating, 57, 62–63, 74; on language difficulties, 100; on life in U.S., 95–96; on meatpacking plant, 115, 125–26, 127; on physical stress of work, 125–26; religion and, 81–83, 84–85; on *traje*, 3

Kaqla, 8, 46, 141, 143n1chap1
K'iche', 1
kinship networks, xii; *vs.* individualism, 69–70, 93; poverty reinforcing, 70; role of, in migration, xxiii, 57, 65–66, 68, 114; in U.S., 134
Konojel, 46

Ladinos: definition of, 42, 143n2intro; language and, 18; Mayans dressing as, 8
land access, 65
language: challenges, 97–105, 143n1chap1; generation gaps in, 97–98; humiliation and, 100; and immigration, xii, 18, 92, 118, 125, 135; and

lack of access to education, 16–18; and trilingual communication, xxiv
Latino population, 129–36; having children, 132; home-ownership among, 135, 138; leadership of, 133, 137; in Nebraska, 130, 131–32; in U.S., 129–30
law enforcement, language issues and, 98–99
Lexington, NE, 130, 132
liberation theology, 86
libraries, 135
limpieza (cleansing), 10–11
literacy, adult, 102
Little Priest Tribal College, xvii
loneliness, 61
López, Mark Hugo, 129
Lucía, xx, 138; on border crossing, 63–64; on corn, 104–5; as domestic servant, 15–16; early life of, 9, 10–11; family of, 63–64, 95; happiness of, 95; on health insurance, 93–94; on language difficulties, 100–101; law enforcement and, 98–99; on meatpacking plants, 115, 126, 128; on physical stress of work, 126; on poverty, 22–25

machista culture, 14
mad cow disease, 127–28
Mam, 1, 18
Manuela, xx, 138; on crossing borders, 73–74; on deciding to immigrate, 56–57, 62; dreams of, for future, 95; family of, 89–91; and Guillermo, 89, 90, 95; on meatpacking plants, 115; on poverty, 25; on *traje*, 3, 7
María, xx; Ann meeting, 54–56; early life of, 10, 55–56; on eating in restaurants, 93; on education, 18–19, 21; on employment, 115–16; on family, 72–73; on immigrating, 58–61, 71–73; on joy of working, 126–27; on languages, 99–100; on life in U.S., 96; as Maricruz, 116; on marriage, 72–73, 76; on poverty,

María, xx (*continued*)
26–27; on religion, 84, 89; on *traje*, 4
market day, 11
marriage: age at, 13; Mayan customs of,
76; not legalized in U.S., 72–73, 76
Martha. *See* González, Martha Florinda
Mary, Saint, xxvi
mat, xii, 143n2pref
Matthew (Catholic priest), 88, 89, 91,
95, 97
The Maya (Coe), 2
Mayan cosmology, xxiv, xxvi–xxvii,
4–5, 140–41
Mayan dress. *See traje* (Mayan dress)
Mayan immigrants. *See also* Latino
population: adaptive skills of, 7–8,
61–62, 92, 103; Anglos' perception
of, xviii; Ann's discovery of, xvii–
xviii; attitudes of, toward Americans,
101; changing Roman Catholicism,
88–89; children of, as Americans,
xxvii–xxviii, 7; children of, left in
Guatemala, xxiii, 13, 69–71, 74, 77,
145n1, 146n13; children's well-being as
priority of, xx, 13, 58, 92–93; contributing to U.S. society, xviii; cultural
practices of, xii, xxiv, xxvii, 1–14, 21–
22, 45, 76, 81–83, 87, 88–89; desiring
understanding, xii–xiii; effects of, on
Nebraska communities, 103–4, 130–
36, 138; family dynamics of, 91–97;
growing food, 134; identities of, protected, xxi; isolation of, 93, 138; leaders among, 99, 137; Mayan-Nebraska
community vision of, xxiv, 135, 137,
140; optimism of, 77, 146n13; post-
traumatic stress of, 40–42, 45, 121–22;
questioning traditions, 14; religious
faith of, 77, 78–79, 81–97; returning
to Guatemala, 138–39, 140; silences
of, 45; starting families in U.S., 73;
undocumented, xxi, xxiii, 56–57, 66–
67, 76, 96, 116–17, 121–22, 134, 136
Mayan languages, xii, 2, 143n1chap1,

144n7chap1; as *dialecto*, 1; masses in,
82; pastoral care in, 88–89
Mayan People's Union (UPMAG), 46
Mayan spirituality, 81–88; denigra-
tion of, 83–84, 85–86; reclaiming, 87;
wordless prayer of, 84
meatpacking plants. *See also* beef industry: advertising in Mexico, 114; conditions in, 107–11, 123–26; conflict at,
118, 122–23; demographics of, 109, 113–
15; documentation status at, 116–17;
duress of work at, 119, 125–26; export
and, 110, 113; funding classes and services, 103, 119, 120; harassment at, 122–
23; history of, 112–13; injuries at, 124;
interpreters for, 114, 117–18, 125; lay-
offs at, 128; in Nebraska cities, xi–xii,
105, 130–36; noise level of, 107, 108, 123;
pay at, 97, 111, 113–14, 124, 127; tour of,
107–11; turnover at, 114, 119; worker
comfort in, 107, 126; worker orientation at, 117–18; and workers, reciprocal
need of, 120; workers' hours at, 127–
28; workers' rights in, xxiv, 118, 122–26
mechanization, 105, 113, 119
medical care: in Guatemala, 22–23;
and health insurance, 93–94; in the
U.S, 94
Memory of Silence (Historical Clarification Commission report), xxiii
Menchú, Rigoberta, xxvi–xxvii, 141;
on gender, 13, 21–22; on *Ladinos*, 42;
Nieta de los mayas, 5, 143n1chap1
methodology, xviii–xxiv, 32–33; empa-
thy and, 83
Metropolitan Community College
(MCC), xvii, 48–49
Mexico: conditions in, affecting migration, 130; and Mexicans in U.S., 132;
profiting off of migrants, 59, 62
La Migra (ICE), 76. *See also* immigration officials
military service: as economic opportunity, 27, 33; human rights abuses in,

CPSIA information can be obtained
at www.ICGtesting.com
Printed in the USA
LVHW03s2047251018
594822LV00001B/43/P